Christopher Oxford

JOHN KEATS

JOHN KEATS

by

MIRIAM ALLOTT

Edited by Ian Scott-Kilvert

PUBLISHED FOR
THE BRITISH COUNCIL
BY LONGMAN GROUP LTD

LONGMAN GROUP LTD
Longman House, Burnt Mill, Harlow, Essex

*Associated companies, branches and
representatives throughout the world*

First published 1976
© Miriam Allott 1976

*Printed in England by
Bradleys, Reading and London*

ISBN 0 582 01257 0

CONTENTS

¶ JOHN KEATS was born in London on 31 October 1795. He died in Rome on 23 February 1821.

JOHN KEATS

I. INTRODUCTION

JOHN KEATS was born in London on 31 October 1795 and died of tuberculosis in Rome, where he had been sent for recovery, on 23 February 1821, having been unable to write any poetry during the last fourteen months because of his illness. His brief poetic career falls roughly into four stages: 1816–17, when he wrote most of the thirty-three poems in his first collection; 1817, when he was chiefly engaged in writing *Endymion;* 1818, a year bringing crucial personal experiences which deeply affected his imagination and which closed with his first attempts at *Hyperion;* and 1819, when he wrote his major poems. The precipitating events of 1818 included his parting with his brother George, who emigrated to America early in 1818; his loss of his other brother, Tom, who died of tuberculosis in the December, aged nineteen; his first sight, during his summer walking tour with his friend Charles Brown, of the dramatic mountain scenery in the Lake District and Scotland; and his introduction in the autumn to Fanny Brawne, the girl he loved and whom he was unable to marry, first because they lacked means and later because he was in any case too ill. He had little longer in which to discover his individual poetic voice and learn something of his craft than many students need to study for a first Arts degree in a British University, but he lived to see published his two collections, *Poems* (1817) and *Lamia, Isabella, The Eve of St Agnes and other Poems* (1820) and, in the interval of these, his lengthy *Endymion: a Poetic Romance* (1818). Much of the rest of his work, including a selection of his remarkable letters, appeared posthumously in two small volumes published in 1848 by Richard Monckton Milnes as *Life, Letters and Literary Remains of John Keats.* Milnes added to these in 1856 by printing for the first time *The Fall of Hyperion,* a reworking of the earlier unfinished *Hyperion.*

The total output is not large and its quality is uneven, but it became a seminal influence for other poets in the nineteenth

century, remains widely familiar today, even if only by hear-
say, and receives from modern scholars the serious critical
attention given to major writers. It is the product of a young
talent wholly dedicated to its poetic calling and to poetry as
a supreme expression of the beautiful, approaching perfection only with the writer's approach to maturity: this was
a state reached, as Keats saw it, by growing away from un-
reflecting delight in external nature into a wise understanding
of the harsher realities of existence and the annihilation of
self-regarding impulses through empathic identification with
others. This he called 'Negative Capability' and associated
above all with the Shakespearian creative imagination. He
did not reach it in his own poetry, though the quick human
intelligence and breadth of feeling in his letters make us
think that with time he might have done so. But he constantly sought to further the dual development of his poetic
and his personal self by working hard at his craft, experi-
menting with different genres and metrical structures, sub-
mitting himself to various literary influences and searching
for a balance between what he called 'sensations'—responsiveness to the concrete particulars of life—and 'thoughts', that
is the exercise of his powers of intellect and understanding and
the nourishing of them by wide reading and varied personal
experience. If we look in turn (as this essay seeks to do) at his
first collection of verse, his narrative poems, his major odes,
his final effort to forge a new kind of poetic statement by
reworking his abortive 'epic', *Hyperion*, into a highly
personal 'vision', and certain passages in his letters, we can
make out, at least in outline, the movements of this self-
discipline and something of the quality of the work it helped
to produce. Critical judgements of Keats have sometimes
been drawn out of true, partly because the human appeal of
an existence haunted by poverty and fatal disease, but finding
compensation in the activity of a vivid creative intelligence,
can distract attention from the work to the life (the tendency
is still common in some modern studies of the Brontë sisters).
In Keats it encouraged the legendary image of a chlorotic
youth too sensitive to withstand hardship and done to death
by hostile reviewers. Readers fastened on passages which sug-
gested exclusively the poet of luxurious 'sensations' and

6

exquisite longing for death, a habit which encouraged a simplistic view of Romanticism in general and of this writer's Romanticism in particular. It became easy to isolate Keats's confession in the 'Ode to a Nightingale',

> many a time
> I have been half in love with easeful Death,
> Called him soft names in many a musèd rhyme,
> To take into the air my quiet breath,
> Now more than ever seems it rich to die,
> To cease upon the midnight with no pain,   (stanza 6)

to overlook his recognition that death, after all, means insentience,

> Still wouldst thou sing, and I have ears in vain—
> To thy high requiem become a sod,   (stanza 6)

and with this to ignore the entire movement of thought and feeling which at first carries the poet from 'The weariness, the fever and the fret' into an ideal world of beauty and permanency and finally returns him to what is actual and inescapable. This curve of feeling shapes in some degree all Keats's major poetry. It is connected with that side of his creative temper where a flexible intelligence seeks to penetrate feeling with the vitality which certain Victorian readers anticipated modern criticism in recognizing. An arresting instance is William Howitt's remark, in a book published in 1847, that Keats's poetry was 'a vivid orgasm of the intellect'. David Masson, in his long article of November 1860 for *Macmillan's Magazine* (he was then its editor) saw as outstanding in Keats 'the universality of his sensuousness', but found the true sign of poetic greatness in the evidence, even in early poems, 'of that power of reflective and constructive intellect by which alone so abundant a wealth of the sensual element could have been ruled and shaped into artistic literary forms'.

    This 'potentiality' adds to our difficulties. In longer lived and more prolific writers we can follow the individual imagination developing in accordance with its own laws of growth and movement. In Keats we catch little more than a glimpse of these laws and of how they might have come to

7

order and direct his work. Had he lived he would probably have suppressed or destroyed a great many early poems and, judging by certain comments in his letters, perhaps even some of those we most admire. As it is we have to understand a talent which made many false starts; produced hundreds of journeyman lines; took time to shake off the insipidities of various unfortunate adoptive styles (especially the current neo-Elizabethanisms most damagingly influential in Leigh Hunt); and produced only a handful of fully achieved poems. Among these are 'The Eve of St Agnes' and the major odes of 1819, one or two unfinished works which paradoxically convey a sense of fine poetic accomplishment, notably the first *Hyperion* and (on a different scale) 'The Eve of St Mark', and a few passages elsewhere—outstandingly the description of Moneta in *The Fall of Hyperion*—which hint at the approach of a new poetic maturity. But we must remember that outside poets of the very first rank, and perhaps even here too, there is in the canon a relatively small area where the shadow falling between conception and execution is dispelled by a high noon of creative intensity. Keats had his own feelings about the not fully achieved work of art as early as March 1817 when, at the age of twenty-one, he wrote a sonnet on first seeing the Elgin Marbles, the celebrated sculptures from the Parthenon brought to England by Lord Elgin and bought for the nation in 1816, when they were housed in the British Museum. 'I never cease to wonder at all that incarnate delight,' he once said, when he was discovered gazing at them with his customary intentness.

> My spirit is too weak—mortality
>   Weighs heavily upon me like unwilling sleep,

he begins, expressing in the sonnet his baffled consciousness of his own artistic inadequacy, his longing to overcome it and the 'dim-conceivèd glories of the brain', which 'Bring round the heart an indescribable feud'. 'These wonders', broken but still withstanding the erosions of time, irradiate the imagination with gleams of something greater than either he or they, in their present form, can convey. They mysteriously mingle,

Grecian grandeur with the rude
Wasting of old Time, with a billowy main,
A sun, a shadow of a magnitude.

The nineteenth-century architect, C. R. Cockerell, contemplating in 1823 Michelangelo's unfinished tondo of the Holy Family, found it 'striking in its unfinished state . . . the subject seems growing from the marble and emerging into life . . . you trace and watch its birth from the sculptor's mind . . .'. A similar sense of emergent power distinguishes the 'shadow of a magnitude' in Keats's unfinished *Hyperions* and the individual intelligence struggling to realize itself in the 1819 odes and the vivacious letters. We cannot scrutinize in this short essay what is 'classical' and what 'romantic', but Keats's writings remind us that incompleteness is a characteristic of one kind of Romantic art. The aesthetic experience offered suggests 'nature naturing', *natura naturans*, rather than 'nature natured', *natura naturata*, which affords another kind of experience, one which we might be forgiven for identifying in this brief epitome with what is 'classical'.

II. EARLY YEARS AND POEMS (1817)

The prelude to Keats's poetic career runs from his birth in 1795—Carlyle was born that year, which should remind us that Keats would have been a man in his forties at the time of the Oxford Movement, the last flare-up of Chartism and Matthew Arnold's first volume of poems—to 1815, when he entered Guy's Hospital as a medical student: he had left his Enfield school in 1811 to be apprenticed to Thomas Hammond, a surgeon and apothecary of Edmonton. The events of a writer's life sometimes seem in retrospect to be designed exclusively for the needs of his creative imagination. Certainly Keats's early years already suggest a necessary 'set'. On one side is the schoolboy, small in height—Keats was always rueful about his want of inches—and sensitive to hurt, who yet was robust, affectionate and mettlesome; there are stories of his squaring up to boys who bullied his brothers and his

9

routing of a butcher's boy who was cruel to a cat. On the other side are the experiences which constantly tested these qualities: fatal family illnesses, deaths, separations, material losses. His father, an ostler at a local inn, died in an accident in 1804; his mother, for whom he felt deeply, in 1810—she remarried shortly after being widowed, and six years later died of the tuberculosis which killed his brother Tom in 1818. His grandmother, who since 1804 had cared for the three brothers and their young sister Fanny (the recipient of some of Keats's gayest and most tender letters), died in 1814. By this time Keats was away at Hammond's and George— Tom accompanied him later—was taken on as a clerk by Richard Abbey, one of the two guardians appointed for the young family. Their latest loss brought more financial hardship because Abbey seemingly was slow to hand over money placed in trust for them. At this stage, though, he did no worse than keep on George and Tom, take Fanny into his home and continue in the belief that he had secured a good professional opening for his eldest ward.

Keats's true calling announced itself in 1814 at the end of his eighteenth year when, fired by *The Faerie Queene* and 'enamoured of its stanza', he composed his first known poem, 'Imitation of Spenser'; the calling was confirmed in March 1817 when C. & J. Ollier published his *Poems* and set the seal on his abandonment of medicine for poetry. In intervals of walking the wards at Guy's Hospital, attending lectures and passing, in July 1816, his qualifying examinations at Apothecary's Hall, he wrote most of the thirty-three poems in the collection. They reflect little of his student life except the loneliness and oppression he felt on leaving the Edmonton countryside to live in lodgings in the crowded capital.

> O Solitude, if I must with thee dwell,
>   Let it not be among the jumbled heap
>   Of murky buildings,   (1–3)

he writes in a sonnet of 1815, picturing the wooded places

>   where the deer's swift leap
> Startles the wild bee from the foxglove bell.   (7–8)

These two lines, with their Wordsworthian ring, are the best in this youthful piece, but it is momentous as his first published work. Its appearance in Leigh Hunt's *The Examiner* for 5 May 1816 signalled his entry into the literary world.

Hunt, whom Keats admired not only for his verses but also for his liberal idealism and his admirable periodical (it served Keats as a kind of Open University), had been a hero since schooldays. The 1817 volume is suffused with his influence and opens with a dedicatory sonnet rejoicing that though 'Glory and loveliness have passed away', the author can feel,

> a free,
> A leafy luxury, seeing I could please
> With these poor offerings a man like thee.   (12–19)

The first of the book's three sections consists of eleven poems, usually saluting in Hunt's sugary style the 'Spenserian' delights of chivalric love and a natural world filled with 'leafy luxury', white-handed nymphs and 'bowery' glades designed for poetic reverie. Two pieces, 'Specimen of an Induction to a Poem' and 'Calidore', inspired by Hunt's tripping style in *The Story of Rimini* (1816), are Keats's abortive first attempts at narrative poetry. Of the three verse epistles in pentameter couplets in the second section, 'To my Brother George' and 'To Charles Cowden Clarke', composed in autumn 1816, show an advance on the earlier and more flowery 'To George Felton Mathew', addressed to a poetaster associate of still more youthful days. (Clarke was the estimable schoolmaster and friend who fostered Keats's early enthusiasm for poetry and introduced his poems to the Hunt circle.) They emulate Hunt's informal verse letters recently published in *The Examiner* but, as elsewhere in the volume, are distinguished by the intermittent accents of an individual voice struggling for expression.

> With shattered boat, oar snapped, and canvas rent
> I slowly sail, scarce knowing my intent,   (17–18)

says Keats despondently in the epistle to Clarke, but his manner gathers buoyancy as he recalls the poetry which his friend taught him:

The grand, the sweet, the terse, the free, the fine;
What swelled with pathos, and what right divine;
Spenserian vowels that elope with ease,
And float along like birds o'er summer seas . . .   (54–7)

In the third section Keats grouped seventeen Petrarchan
sonnets, mostly celebrating recent literary friendships and
artistic enthusiasms, among them 'On seeing the Elgin
Marbles', 'Great spirits now on earth are sojourning . . .',
which praises Hunt, Wordsworth and the painter Benjamin
Haydon, and 'On first looking into Chapman's Homer',
unquestionably the finest performance of this early period.
He closed the volume with his reflective, confessional 'Sleep
and Poetry', running to some four hundred lines in pentameter couplets and linked with 'I stood tip-toe upon a little
hill . . .', written in the same metre and printed in his first
section. Unequal in quality and awkward in meeting the
simultaneous demands of sense, syntax and rhyme, these
nevertheless foreshadow later achievements. 'I stood tip-
toe . . .' is a first gesture towards *Endymion*. Foremost among
nature's 'luxuries' which quicken poetic inspiration is the
moon:

O Maker of sweet poets, dear delight
Of this fair world.   (116–17)

It was 'a poet, sure a lover too' who, from his post on Mount
Latmus,

Wept that such beauty should be desolate.
So in fine wrath some golden sounds he won
And gave meek Cynthia her Endymion.   (202–4)

Touched by Wordsworth's account of Diana, Apollo and
other rural deities in Book IV of *The Excursion*, which was a
profoundly influential work for the second generation of
Romantic poets, Keats too finds that myths originate in
imaginative response to the beauties of nature and singles out
the haunting legends of Eros and Psyche (141–50), Pan and
Syrinx (157–62) and Narcissus and Echo (163–80). The theme
recurs in 'Sleep and Poetry', which brings together for the

first time central ideas concerning the interdependence of sleep, reverie and poetic creativity; the vitalizing of the natural world through classical myth; and individual progress from what Keats later termed, in a famous letter of May 1818 to John Hamilton Reynolds, the 'Chamber of Maiden-Thought' to the darker world of 'Misery and Heartbreak, Pain, Sickness and oppression'. 'Byron says "knowledge is Sorrow"', reflects Keats in the same letter, 'and I go on to say "Sorrow is Wisdom".' The influence from Wordsworth's 'Tintern Abbey', working upon his own views about personal development, mitigates to some degree the debilitating prettinesses of his poetic language.

> Oh, for ten years, that I may overwhelm
> Myself in poesy   (96–7)

he writes, looking for the time when simple delight in 'the realm of Flora and old Pan' will yield to,

> a nobler life
> Where I may find the agonies, the strife
> Of human hearts—   (123–5)

He conjures up an image of the creative imagination, partly inspired by the portrayal in certain of Poussin's paintings of a chariot driven across the sky by Apollo, who was always an immensely potent figure for him. A charioteer descends to earth and communes with nature, but then focuses on the 'shapes of delight, of mystery, and fear' embodied in the procession of men and women now passing before him. The conception is sufficiently striking but ultimately eludes his poetic reach. At this stage of his career, the distance between Keats's available resources and his high sense of poetic vocation begins to narrow when he frees his language from its fustian clutter by concentrating on 'the object as in itself it is': in 'To Charles Cowden Clarke' the moon seen among clouds,

> As though she were reclining in a bed
> Of bean blossoms, in heaven freshly shed,   (95–6)

the uneven sound of Clarke's parting footsteps at night, sometimes resonant on the 'gravelly' path, sometimes muffled as he stepped on the grass verge; or the attaching particularity found in his sonnet 'To my Brothers',

> Small, busy flames play through the fresh-laid coals,
> And their faint cracklings o'er our silence creep,

and felt again in his description of setting out at night after the warm gathering at Hunt's Hampstead cottage,

> Keen, fitful gusts are whispering here and there,
> Among the bushes, half leafless and dry;
> The stars look very cold about the sky,
> And I have many miles on foot to fare.

The clarity and immediacy usually peter out too soon but the promise of poetic vigour is sustained in the Chapman sonnet, where the creative imagination as a 'golden' realm filled with 'wonders' generates the poem's unifying imagery of exploration and discovery and for once (it was long before this happened again), the poem's structure and style are consistent with its movement of thought and feeling. Keats wrote the poem rapidly one October night in 1816 after he and Clarke had spent many hours poring excitedly for the first time over Chapman's translation of Homer. (Homer had been familiar to them hitherto only in Pope's version, which never afforded Keats the keen delight he found, for instance, in his favourite line from Chapman on Odysseus shipwrecked: 'The sea had soaked his heart through . . .'). In another sonnet of the period, 'How many bards gild the lapses of time!', Keats records the 'thronging' in his mind of recollections from his favourite poets, which make 'a pleasing harmony' like the mingling of evening sounds— birdsong, 'the whispering of the leaves', 'the voice of waters' —as they lose their individual identity in the distance. This sonnet vividly describes the working of his densely associative literary memory, and the Chapman sonnet is a rare early illustration of his successful 'alchemizing' of these recollections into his own idiom. It draws on wide literary memories, many of them probably half-conscious, some gathered from contemporary authors (Wordsworth included) and most of them echoed from his schoolroom reading: the most influential were accounts, in William Robertson's *History of America*, of Balboa, Cortez and the discovery of gold in the New World, and, in a schoolbook on astronomy, of the first sighting by Herschell in 1781 of the planet Uranus. The individual instances in the sestet of man's encounters with dazzling new experience and knowledge reinforce the fine opening breadth of the octave. Leigh Hunt celebrated the 'prematurely masculine' vein in this 'noble sonnet', which closed 'with so energetic a calmness and which completely announced the new poet taking possession'.

III. NARRATIVE POEMS

With his first volume of poems in print, Keats devoted the rest of the year to *Endymion*, the 'Poetic Romance' which was to be 'a test, a trial of my Powers of Imagination and chiefly of my invention by which I must make 4,000 lines out of one bare circumstance', the 'circumstance' being the legend that the moon goddess—known variously in classical myth as Diana, Phoebe and Cynthia—fell in love with the shepherd Endymion as he lay asleep on the mountain heights of Caria. For his first major literary enterprise Keats obeyed the narrative impulse which prompted his fragmentary Huntian-Spenserian tales in 1816 and led him, in 1819, to compose 'The Eve of St Agnes', 'La Belle Dame Sans Merci' and the more ambitious and unequal 'Lamia'. But, as A. C. Bradley saw in his *Oxford Lectures on Poetry* (1909), the 'long poem' in the Romantic period, adding its weight to a progressive break-down of genres, contains lyrical, confessional and reflective elements, as well as a narrative interest. Keats usually relates a love story which expresses personal ideas and feelings rather more urgently than it arouses interest in 'what happens next' to the love-lorn characters. *Endymion* uninhibitedly dramatizes his current aspirations for the supreme experience of an ideal passion. Later (as with Yeats who met Maud Gonne after celebrating the legendary Niamh in *The Wanderings of Oisin*) his relationship with what he called in 'Lamia' a 'real woman' gave his work a new emotional charge. 'The Eve of St Agnes' was written in January–February 1819, a few weeks after his first 'understanding' with Fanny Brawne on Christmas Day, and celebrates the warmth of a requited passion, but characteristically cannot forget its attendant hazards nor its vulnerability to time. His young brother had just died, and love and death are inextricably bound together in his imagination. In 'La Belle Dame Sans Merci' and 'Lamia', written respectively on 21 April and between about 28 June and 5 September in the same year, where the destructiveness of passion is expressed as keenly as its delight, the emotion is still more ambivalent and the presence of death a yet more haunting presence. The earlier 'Isabella, or the Pot of Basil', on the other hand, written during March to April 1818, before the most overwhelming personal experiences of that year, is in spite of its authorial interpolations the least 'personal' of these love stories and led Keats a step or two along a road not taken elsewhere in his poetic life.

All these poems are consciously exploratory in their diverse techniques and source materials. *Endymion* continues in the pentameter couplets used for its precursor, 'I stood tip-toe . . .', but Keats handles *ottava rima* for his Italian 'Isabella', Spenserians for 'The Eve of St Agnes', ballad style quatrains for 'La Belle Dame Sans Merci', seven-syllabled couplets for the fragmentary 'The Eve of St Mark' and Drydenesque couplets for 'Lamia'. The first and last draw on classical, the rest on medieval sources. The latter suited his liking for rich pictorial effects and, as it turned out, provided themes which allowed him to balance the inner and the outer, so the work may be quickened by personal feeling without falling into disabling subjectivity.

Endymion, with more flats than elevations in its four long Books, which here we can only glance at in passing, is for many readers a monument of misdirected effort. But its general style is an improvement on *Poems* (1817), reflecting (as in the fine April 1817 sonnet 'On the Sea') the first effects of his simultaneous disenchantment with Hunt and renewed passion for Shakespeare, whom he now saw as his 'Presider'. Some passages, especially the Hymn to Pan in Book I, which is his first major ode (the Ode to Sorrow in Book IV is less distinguished), look forward to the work of 1819. New ground is broken in his use of a narrative medium to express current ideas about human experience, while his poetic creativity is stimulated afresh by his 'thronging' literary recollections, now chiefly from Sandys's *Ovid* and classical reference books 'devoured' (as Clarke put it) at school; allusions to Endymion and the moon in the Elizabethans, particularly Shakespeare, Spenser and Drayton; and details of magical journeys from *The Arabian Nights* and colourful modern verse narratives including Landor's *Gebir* (1798) and Southey's two lengthy poems, *Thalaba the Destroyer* (1801) and *The Curse of Kehana* (1810). The hero's journeys—he seeks the shining amorous girl of his dream vision on the earth (Book I), beneath it (Book II), under the sea (Book III) and in the air (Book IV)—rework the stages of individual development outlined in 'Sleep and Poetry'. From his carefree existence among his native woods and hills, he passes into melancholy obsession with the difference between the ideal and the actual and is finally admitted to unshadowed bliss only after learning selfless identification with the pain of others. Since love appears in this poem as the supreme good, its frustration here is the type of all pain. Endymion's succouring of Glaucus and the drowned lovers in Book III and his sacrifice of his 'dream' for the love-lorn Indian maid in Book IV ensure the transformation of this dusky girl into his fair divinity (this has in context a startling and somewhat perfunctory effect which suggests the author's growing fatigue), who now summons him to share with her 'an immortality of passion'.

The poem follows too many side-winds of inspiration to qualify as a sustained allegory, as it is sometimes mistakenly described, but the ordering of the story implies—perhaps as an answer to Shelley's gloomy 'Alastor' (1816)—that the ideal is indeed attainable, provided one first enters into and accepts the bliss and bale of everyday life. This suggestion is strengthened by the famous 'pleasure-thermometer' passage in Book I (777–842) tracing the gradations of human happiness, which rise from delight in nature and art to the human ties of friendship and, supremely, physical love. The driving force throughout is man's longing for 'fellowship with essence' by which he will ultimately

> shine
> Full alchemized, and free of space.   (I, 779–80)

The mystery of an ultimate knowledge, felt but not realizable in words, is conveyed in the 'Hymn to Pan', where the god of universal nature is invoked as the 'unimaginable lodge/For solitary thinkings' which

> dodge
> Conception to the very bourne of heaven.   (I, 294–5)

The lines anticipate the 'silent form' in the 'Ode on a Grecian Urn' which teases the poet

> out of thought
> As doth eternity. . . .   (44–5)

Keats's fine Preface shows that he judged *Endymion's* immaturity, which is very noticeable in its boyishly succulent love scenes, more penetratingly than its many unfriendly reviewers in the Tory periodicals, who disliked him on principle as a member of the 'Cockney' school associated with Leigh Hunt. He found similar weaknesses in 'Isabella'—'what I should call were I a reviewer "A weak-sided poem"'—and in 'The Eve of St Agnes', only 'not so glaring', but thought 'Lamia' was stronger and had more 'fire'. His readers generally take a different view: 'Isabella' is flawed but represents an advance from adolescence to adulthood;[1] 'The Eve of St Agnes' imaginatively blends with its sumptuous Elizabethan opulence individual feeling for what has 'no joy, nor love, nor light'; while 'Lamia', with some highly accomplished versification to its credit, uneasily mingles virtuoso pictorial effects, intense feeling and would-be sophisticated satire, a mode in which Keats was never at home, as the quasi-Byronic 'The Cap and Bells', also of late 1819, unhappily demonstrates at some length.

It can be argued that Keats's need to assimilate the experiences of 1818 and 1819 worked as much against as for his success in narrative poetry. 'Isabella', which hints at the

[1] See F. W. Bateson, *English Poetry*, 1950, p. 222 *n.*

possibility of a different kind of achievement, was written before George's departure, Tom's death and the arrival in his life of Fanny Brawne, and was undertaken in obedience to a 'public' impulse, that is the suggestion in Hazlitt's February 1818 lecture, 'On Dryden and Pope', that modern translations of Boccaccio's tales 'as that of Isabella' might win a popular success. It is less poised than its successor, 'The Eve of St Agnes', and matches *Endymion* in its lush love scenes and awkward attempts at naturalistic dialogue. 'Those lips, O slippery blisses', says Keats in *Endymion* and now Lorenzo's lips 'poesy' with Isabella's 'in dewy rhyme'. 'Goodbye! I'll soon be back' is one of several bathetic touches in the lovers' conversation, and the rhodomontade in the stanzas castigating Isabella's brothers, who kill Lorenzo because he is too poor, is out of keeping with the fine plangency in the rest of the tale. But Keats's modern fellow poet, Edward Thomas, praised the *ottava rima* stanzas, with their 'adagio' effect, for making 'Isabella' appropriately, 'a very still poem' and for accommodating better than his early couplets Keats's 'choiceness of detail'. Thomas could have added that this detail is now more purposefully employed to focus both the events in the narrative and the feelings they generate. The dead Lorenzo, appearing to Isabella in a dream, mourns his lost love and the small touching sounds of life in the world she inhabits. The chestnut leaves and 'prickly nuts' fall onto his grave, a 'sheep-fold bleat' reaches him from beyond the river, he hears 'the glossy bees at noon . . . fieldward pass', but

> Those sounds grow strange to me,
> And thou art distant in humanity. (stanza 39)

The 'immortality of passion' sought in *Endymion* yields to another order of feeling,

> Thy beauty grows upon me, and I feel
> A greater love through all my essence steal. (stanza 40)

A year later, in 'The Eve of St Agnes', Keats's growing concentration on 'the object as in itself it is' seems for most of the story to be at the service of a less universalizing vision, but the hostile setting, which includes Madeline's family who play Capulet to Porphyro's Montague, the bleak winter and rising storm and the chill of age and death stiffening the figures of the Beadsman and old Angela, provides an oblique commentary on the stolen night in Madeline's room, where Keats introduces his richest 'luxuries' yet, exquisitely indulging the senses with music, delicacies from 'silken Samarkand to cedared Lebanon' and a love effortlessly consummated in a dream where the actual and the ideal 'melt' deliciously into one another. This interplay of warmth and cold, colour and paleness, love and death, constitute the poem's 'criticism of life', this time, it seems (since Madeline escapes with Porphyro to his home 'over the moors'), with a measured optimism about reaching a longed-for good here and now. But the oppositions suggest a more restless preoccupation with the difference between ideal and actual experience than one might have expected after the touching quietude briefly achieved in 'Isabella'. Technically, Keats is no less at home with his Spenserian stanzas than with his *ottava rima*, commanding in them the peculiarly rich pictorial details which enliven his improvisation on the 'popular superstition' that a girl who goes fasting to bed on St Agnes's Eve will see her future husband in a dream. The medieval colouring, which is more lavish than in 'The Eve of St Mark', the unfinished poem which William Morris saw as a main inspiration behind the Victorian Pre-Raphaelite movement, paradoxically owes much to contemporary rather than earlier writers, especially Scott's *The Lay of the Last Minstrel* (1805), Mrs Radcliffe's 'Gothick' tales and Coleridge's 'Christabel' (1816). It owes something, too, to Keats's recent visits to Chichester Cathedral and the newly established chapel at Stansted. Of course the family feud and the role of Madeline's aged attendant Angela come straight from *Romeo and Juliet*, one of the many plays densely marked in his copy of Shakespeare now lodged at Hampstead.

It is impossible to represent adequately here the textural richness nourished by these currents of literary and personal experience, but the following is an instance of the contrasts between warmth and encompassing cold which make the poem something more than a pretty piece of medievalism

inspired by wishful erotic fantasy. The Beadsman, 'meagre,
barefoot, wan', opens the poem, returning after prayer along
'the chapel aisle'—

> The sculptured dead, on each side, seemed to freeze,
> Imprisoned in black, purgatorial rails . . .   (stanza 2)

—and his death ends it,

> The Beadsman, after thousand aves told,
> For aye unsought for slept among his ashes cold.
>
>   (stanza 42)

In the interval are the events in Madeline's room, which open
with the hidden Porphyro secretly watching her say her
prayers and prepare for bed, a description much worked over
in the manuscript (the self-criticism revealed by Keats's
habits of revision is a subject on its own). The final version,
with its suggestions of warmth, youth and physical immediacy, marvellously counterpoints the aged Beadsman's
solitary devotions and his approaching death:

> Full on this casement shone the wintry moon,
> And threw warm gules on Madeline's fair breast
> As down she knelt for heaven's grace and boon;
> Rose-bloom fell on her hands, together pressed,
> And on her silver cross soft amethyst,
> And on her hair a glory, like a saint.
> She seemed a splendid angel, newly dressed,
> Save wings, for Heaven. Porphyro grew faint;
> She knelt, so pure a thing, so free from mortal taint.

> Anon his heart revives; her vespers done,
> Of all its wreathèd pearls her hair she frees;
> Unclasps her warmèd jewels one by one;
> Loosens her fragrant bodice; by degrees
> Her rich attire creeps rustling to her knees.
> Half-hidden, like a mermaid in sea-weed,
> Pensive awhile she dreams awake, and sees,
> In fancy, fair St Agnes in her bed,
> But dares not look behind, or all the charm is fled.
>
>   (stanzas 25, 26)

As I have said elsewhere,[1] in 'La Belle Dame Sans Merci', written a few months later on 21 April 1819, and 'Lamia', written in the September of the same year, when Keats had left London to 'wean' himself from his passion for Fanny so that he could try to make his way with his writing, 'the moderate "wishful" optimism of "The Eve of St Agnes" is rejected for something much more uncompromising. The "knight-at-arms" awakens "on the cold hill side", and Lycius is destroyed. The lady encountered "in the meads", and the "maiden bright" whom Lycius finds "a young bird's flutter from a wood", both turn out to be fatal enchantresses who spell disaster for their victims and are themselves somehow doomed.' Formally, though, there is no similarity between the two narratives. The earlier, perhaps Keats's most magical and self-sufficient poem, is very short, and its austere ballad stanza, forbidding the indulgence of luxuriant detail, relies on compression and spare figurative imagery for emotional effect. The density of imaginative experience which helped to bring this deceptively simple little poem into being makes it barely easier to comment upon in a short space than *Endymion*. But it can be said at once that, in contrast to Keats's earlier narratives, where love is a kind of dream which quickens and delights every sense and is constantly threatened by the hard realities of the ordinary world, the enchantment is now itself a threat and carries from the beginning the seeds of its own destruction. The poem opens, like 'The Eve of St Agnes', with winter images which affect us the more because the absences recall what once existed in a happier season:

> The sedge has withered from the lake,
> And no birds sing!   (stanza 1)

The 'lady' and her enchantment are identified with 'winter' even more than with 'summer' for her thrallèd knights have caught from her an everlasting cold.

> I saw their starved lips in the gloam
> With horrid warning gapèd wide,
> And I awoke, and found me here
> On the cold hill side.   (stanza 11)

---

[1] 'Isabella', 'The Eve of St Agnes' and 'Lamia', in *John Keats: A Reassessment*, ed. K. Muir, 1958 (reprinted 1969), p. 56.

The echoes in the poem arrive most resonantly, perhaps, from Spenser and Chatterton, but the resemblance to the traditional ballad of True Thomas the Rhymer, victim of another enchantress, makes it almost certain that Keats's pre-occupation with the destructiveness of love and the inevitability of death is closely associated with fears for his own poetic destiny. His treatment of his three central characters in the much longer 'Lamia' and his general uncertainty of direction in this poem suggest his continued concern with an increasingly unsettling dilemma. Keats based his new story on an anecdote in Burton's *Anatomy of Melancholy*. Lycius, a student of philosophy and 'twenty-five years of age', is beguiled by a beautiful woman who leads him to her house in Corinth with promises of music, song, feasting and eternal love—the pattern of the Keatsian enchanted dream. They live blissfully until Lycius insists on a public wedding; whereon the philosopher Apollonius appears among the guests, recognizes the lady as an enchantress, 'a serpent, a lamia' and all about her 'like Tantalus's gold . . . no substance, but mere illusions'. In the source, she vanishes 'in an instant', together with her house and everything in it. In the poem the destiny of both lovers is tragic. Lamia has the power 'to unperplex bliss from its neighbour pain' (which the 'dreamer' certainly cannot do, according to the argument in *The Fall of Hyperion*, where he 'vexes mankind'), is herself the victim as well as the caster of spells, and when she is destroyed, Lycius is destroyed too.

> And Lycius' arms were empty of delight,
> As were his limbs of life, from that same night.
> . . .
>   no pulse, or breath they found,
> And, in its marriage robe, the heavy body wound.
> (II, 307–8; 310–11)

Here, then, is the problem posed in the 1819 odes. Where lies the 'truth'? In ideal experience or everyday reality? At the far end of the spectrum from the 'dream' is 'cold Philosophy', though this is not to be confused with the 'wisdom' which Keats elsewhere sees nourished by imaginative response to life and art. Matthew Arnold felt that the Romantic poets 'did not know enough'. This was Keats's worry too. But to 'know enough' might mean exercising processes of ratiocination and abstract thought inimical to the poetic imagination. He had seen in 1817 and early in 1818 that 'a gradual ripening of the intellectual powers' was essential 'for the purposes of great productions' and had felt that the way lay through 'application, study and thought'; at the same time he had always found it difficult to see 'how any thing can be known for truth by consequitive reasoning', hence his vivid simile, 'The Imagination may be compared to Adam's dream—he awoke and found it truth', and his call 'O for a Life of Sensations rather than of Thoughts'. Now, torn between Apollonius' 'consequitive thinking' and the quickening 'sensations' of Lamia's enchanted dream, he produces a poem interesting to dissect thematically but compelling imaginative assent only in relatively few phrases and passages. To set against his awkward shifts of tone and his stylistic gaucheries, especially his attempted worldly manner in describing 'a real woman' as 'a treat' and love as always short-lived,

> Love in a hut, with water and a crust,
> Is—Love, forgive us!—cinders, ashes, dust,   (II, 1–2)

are Hermes seen as 'the star of Lethe'; Lamia described first in her brilliantly marked 'gordian shape . . . rainbow sided, touched with miseries' and later in her quasi-Miltonic transmogrification, 'convulsed with scarlet pain' as she assumes her human form; the ritualistic and inventive construction of her magic palace; and, expanded from a few hints in Burton, the portrait of Corinth,

> And all her populous streets and temples lewd,
> Muttered, like tempest in the distance brewed,
> . . .
> Men, women, rich and poor, in the cool hours
> Shuffled their sandals o'er the pavement white,
> Companioned or alone; while many a light
> Flared, here and there, from wealthy festivals . . .
> (I, 352–8)

The latter makes a first-rate companion piece for the cool and charming account of Bertha's quiet cathedral town in the tantalizingly fragmentary 'The Eve of St Mark':

The city streets were clean and fair
From wholesome drench of April rains,
And, on the western window panes,
The chilly sunset faintly told
Of unmatured green valleys cold,
Of the green thorny bloomless hedge,
Of rivers new with spring-tide sedge,
Of primroses by sheltered rills,
And daisies on the aguish hills.
Twice holy was the Sabbath-bell;
The silent streets were crowded well
With staid and pious companies,
Warm from their fireside orat'ries,
And moving with demurest air
To even-song and vesper prayer.
Each archèd porch, and entry low
Was filled with patient folk and slow,
With whispers hush and shuffling feet,
While played the organ loud and sweet.   (4–22)

IV. THE 1819 ODES

Certain anxieties underlying 'Lamia' became explicit in lines
which Keats wrote for Fanny on their reunion in October
1819. He mourns his lost liberty and the tyranny of a love
which impedes his 'winged' Muse, in earlier days,

> ever ready . . . to take her course
> Whither I bent her force,
> Unintellectual, yet divine to me.
> Divine, I say! What sea-bird o'er the sea
> Is a philosopher the while he goes
> Winging along where the great water throes?
>   (*To* [*Fanny*], 12–17)

But in the interval since 'The Eve of St Agnes' he had written
his famous odes, which could not be what they are without
their 'intellectual' components and the interpenetration in
them of feeling and thought. With Wordsworth's Immortality ode, Milton's Nativity hymn and Coleridge's 'On
Dejection', these are probably the best known odes in

English and they have generated a quantity of critical and scholarly discussion so vast that it is impossible now to compute its scale. Yet Keats singled out the weakest, on Indolence, as the poem he most enjoyed writing in 1819; pushed the manuscript of the 'Ode to a Nightingale' behind some books (whence it was rescued by Charles Brown); and although he copied out or mentioned most of his recent poems in his journal-letters to his brother George in America, only the 'Ode to Psyche' and the 'Ode to Autumn' receive comment. The circumstance adds to the mysteriousness of his achievement in these poems. They display a sudden advance in his mastery of his poetic skills and in his use of them to explore, more concentratedly than in the narratives and with a stronger gnomic effect, the relationship between human suffering, the ideal in art and individual aspiration, and the role of the poet, whose representations of the beautiful and enduring 'tease us out of thought', because we cannot be sure whether they constitute a vision of truth or a wishful dream. At the heart of the odes is the necessity to accept suffering and the transience of youth, beauty and love, and to do so without destroying imaginative order and harmony. Earlier, in the 'Epistle to John Reynolds' written during March 1818, Keats had wished that 'dreams' of poets and painters could take their colouring 'From something of material sublime' rather than from gloomy inner conflict and, longing for wisdom, had grieved that he was too untutored to 'philosophize' without despondency:

> It is a flaw
> In happiness to see beyond our bourn—
> It forces us in summer skies to mourn;
> It spoils the singing of the nightingale.   (82–5)

A year later, in 'Ode to a Nightingale', the singing is not 'spoilt': rather its intense delight sharpens the poet's pain in the everyday world,

> Where youth grows pale, and spectre-thin, and dies,
> Where but to think is to be full of sorrow,   (26–7)

but which still compels a movement of necessary assent. The mental and emotional processes which prepared the way for these poems were reinforced by a bold series of technical experiments. Keats's youthful odes—'To Apollo' is an instance—gesture towards English Pindarics, but his metrical structure in 1819 is entirely new. He evolved his characteristic stanza from long practice with existing sonnet forms. As we have seen, he had a brilliant early success with the Petrarchan kind. He turned after January 1818 to the Shakespearian, which inspired 'When I have fears that I may cease to be . . .' and the 'Bright Star!' sonnet, two of his memorable poems on the Shakespearian themes of love, poetic ambition and the passage of time. But in April 1819 he set about discovering 'a better sonnet stanza than we have', the Petrarchan having too many 'pouncing rhymes', and the Shakespearian being 'too elegiac—and the couplet at the end . . . has seldom a pleasing effect'. His experiments—they include the unrhymed sonnet 'If by dull rhymes our English must be chained . . .' and the understandably often anthologized 'To Sleep'—seem not to have satisfied him. Yet they led to his ode stanza's combination of a 'Shakespearian' quatrain and a 'Petrarchan' sestet and to the form which gave him both discipline and flexibility in a manner removed from the neatly tripping seven-syllabled trochaic couplets he had used for his 'Ode to Fancy' and 'Bards of passion . . .' in the previous December: he gives, though, a hint of his future development in his attractive fragment of an 'Ode to May' written earlier that year.

Keats acknowledged his renewed concern with craftsmanship when he copied out the 'Ode to Psyche' on 30 April in a journal letter, claiming that it was 'the first and only [poem] with which I have taken even moderate pains—I have for the most part dash'd off my lines in a hurry—this I have done leisurely—I think it reads more richly for it'. This is a matter of debate among its readers, though it seems true to say that, just as 'To Autumn' is more complex than the direct statement of reconciliation and acceptance it is often taken to be, so the undertones in Keats's celebration of Psyche make it more interesting than 'a pretty piece of Paganism' (Wordsworth's ill-fitting description of the 'Hymn to Pan'). Keats, we know from his letter, understood that Psyche meant the soul. Elsewhere in the same letter he images the world as 'a vale of soul-making', and its 'pains and troubles' as 'necessary to school an intelligence and make it a soul'. He must have fastened on the resemblance between Psyche's quest for Eros and Endymion's quest for the goddess in his own story, since both are 'schooled' by 'pains and troubles' before reaching 'an immortality of passion'. It is Psyche thus translated whom Keats celebrates, picturing her in his first stanza asleep beside Eros in the lush grass and disappointingly—but unsurprisingly if we accept the association—reverting to the artificial style of *Endymion* ('soft-conchèd ear', 'tender eye-dawn of aurorean love'). Yet it is difficult not to detect in his later stanzas—which recall that she came 'too late' to 'Olympus' faded hierarchy' and so missed 'the happy pieties', the 'antique vows' and 'the fond believing lyre'—mingled tones of regret for the vanished 'worship of a simple day' (the phrase is from the 'Ode to May') and belief that to the 'fond worshippers' Psyche's destiny would mean less than to the hard-pressed poet of a darker age. All the same, Keats's 'pains' serve his themes less than the pictorial effects and the quasi-liturgical incantatory rhythms and repetitions, sometimes echoing Milton's Nativity Ode, which he wanted from his studiedly loose Pindaric form with its irregular verse paragraphs and varying length of line. In the densely worked last stanza, which describes the 'fane' to be built for Psyche in some 'untrodden region of my mind', the emphasis finally shifts from 'the pale-mouth'd prophet dreaming' and returns to an individual idiom, especially in the lines (deeply admired by Ruskin) about the 'dark-clustering pines' which fledge 'the wild-ridged mountains'; the conception of 'the wreath'd trellis of a working brain', which combines with medical recollections Keats's habitual sense of the 'labyrinthine' and 'Daedalian' nature of the creative imagination; and the closing reference to the window open at night 'To let the warm love in', an allusion to Eros now openly visiting Psyche and perhaps also, as at least one critic has thought, to his feelings about Fanny. She was living at this time next door to him in Hampstead and he would have been able to see her lighted window near him at night.

In his next two odes, both of May 1819, Keats 'schools' his intelligence by posing against the 'worlds of pains and sorrows' an object suggesting the possibility of permanence:

in the first the nightingale's song, unchanged from age to age and identified with the beauty of the natural world; in the second an ancient Greek urn, fresh as when the artist made it and on its frieze a depicted world of unchanging youth, love and 'happy piety'. His interrogation determines a poetic structure based on the flight from everyday reality and the return to it, but the 'Ode on a Grecian Urn', because it is more ostensibly a 'dialogue of the mind with itself' about the ambiguous relationship between ideal and actual experience—taken up from its predecessor's final line, 'Fled is that music. Do I wake or sleep?'—possesses wider tonal range with less textural richness. (Keats printed it after the 'Ode to a Nightingale' in his 1820 volume, perhaps as an intended reply.) The new ten-line stanza serves these diverse effects well, though Keats afterwards dropped the short eighth line in the 'Ode to a Nightingale', which was possibly meant to accord with the lyrical movement of the bird's song. The melodic pattern of onomatopoeic effects, worked at with 'pains' in the Psyche ode largely for its own sake, now enacts successive states of feeling: 'drowsy numbness' (a state often prefacing Keats's moods of creativity) induced by excessive pleasure in the bird's song; longing to escape with the singer from 'the weariness, the fever and the fret' into the flower-scented woods; delight in his own lullingly rich evocation of them; and back, through thoughts of death, to the solitary self, grieving at the term set to human happiness and puzzled about the validity of the reverie. Death, at first seemingly a 'luxury', becomes a repellent finality from which only the bird can escape to comfort with its 'self-same song' generations of suffering men and women, 'emperor and clown' alike, and also 'perhaps', in an unforgettable image of loss and exile,

> the sad heart of Ruth, when, sick for home,
> She stood in tears among the alien corn. (66–7)

The celebrated stanza imagining the woods in an early summer night transmutes with the familiar Keatsian alchemy passages about summer sweetness, renewal and growth remembered from other poets (particularly Coleridge's 'To a Nightingale' of 1798 and Shakespeare's 'I know a bank whereon the wild thyme grows') into an individual celebration of nature's 'luxuries' now entangled with thoughts of death. It is in an 'embalmed' darkness that the poet guesses 'each sweet' and summons in his session of silent thought the 'white hawthorn and the pastoral eglantine', the 'fast-fading violets', and

> mid-May's eldest child,
> The coming musk-rose, full of dewy wine,
> The murmurous haunt of flies on summer eves.
>
> (48–50)

This ode questions the validity of the poet's 'fancy' and not the quality of the song that inspires it, but Keats's urn arouses feelings whose ambivalency affects the tone of his celebration, as the effort is made alternately to subdue and define uncertainty. The movement is between contrasts of activity and stillness, warmth and cold, permanency and transience, with the sestet in each of the five stanzas countering or expanding upon the quatrain, which may itself set forward puzzling contrarieties. The opening quatrain defines the 'still' perfection of this Attic *objet d'art*, but the humanizing terms—'unravished bride of quietness', 'foster-child', 'silvan historian'—attend to a paradoxical union of age and youth, the human and the artificial, while the breathless questions of the sestet—

> What men or gods are these? What maidens loth?
> What mad pursuit? What struggle to escape? (8–9)

—clearly no longer suggest stillness. In the second stanza's sestet the figures are now neither vital nor reposed but imprisoned:

> Fair youth beneath the trees, thou canst not leave
> Thy song, nor ever can those trees be bare.

The ostensibly comforting lines,

> She cannot fade, though thou hast not thy bliss,
> For ever wilt thou love and she be fair! (19–20)

from this keen sensitivity to suffering and change he
evolve a statement whose imaginative order provides
stay against impermanence. More explicit than else-
and on another level from his young eroticism in
n, is his use, noticeable in the closing stanza, of
magery as a paradigm for the inextricable relationship
joy and sorrow:

e, in the very temple of Delight
eiled Melancholy has her sovran shrine.

er critic has said,[1] the ensuing lines,

Though seen of none save him whose strenuous tongue
an burst Joy's grape against his palate fine;
soul shall taste the sadness of her might,
And be among her cloudy trophies hung,

a recollection of *Troilus and Cressida*, III, ii, 19–24
y Keats in his copy of Shakespeare),

What will it be
n that the wat'ry palates taste indeed
's thrice-repured nectar? Death, I fear me;
ding destruction; or some joy too fine,
ubtle-potent, tun'd too sharp in sweetness,
ie capacity of my ruder powers,

arallel strengthens the felt presence of sexual
n the stanza. Moreover the curve of feeling,
m the structure of the other odes and also found
ems, which takes the poet from languor to intense
id out of this to another, sadder, and more anti-
tate of being, corresponds to the pattern of Keats's
oetic creativity.
anguor' alone which Keats celebrates in his 'Ode
e'. The poem, not surprisingly, lacks the con-
of the other odes, which were written in obedi-
re urgent creative impulse. Keats, it seems, found
en in deciding on the final arrangement of his
sh, *John Keats*, 1966, p. 147.

recall the antithetical real world in the Nightingale ode,

Where Beauty cannot keep her lustrous eyes,
Or new love pine at them beyond to-morrow,
(29–30)

and lead into the plaintive invocation, 'O happy, happy
love' (the epithet is equally insistent in the two earlier odes),
which convey the total absence of happiness in the poet
himself. Simultaneously the urn becomes remote,

All breathing human passion far above,
That leaves a heart high-sorrowful and cloyed. (28–9)

The entire stanza risks a damaging self-indulgence, from
which Keats rescues himself by the brilliant innovation in his
subsequent sestet which turns from the urn to the 'actual'
world from which its figures came, a 'little town' where
empty streets,

for evermore
Will silent be; and not a soul to tell
Why thou art desolate can e'er return,

a conception alien to the urn's creator but typical of the poet,
who—this time obliquely—leads us back through the terms
'empty' and 'desolate' to his 'sole self'. From this he modulates into his attempted final summary, where the urn at first
becomes no more than an 'Attic shape' covered with 'marble'
—not 'warm' or 'panting'—figures. Yet his first delight still
lingers with his new 'reflective' position, and the entire complex which 'teases us out of thought/As doth eternity' finds
its only possible expressive outlet in the paradox 'Cold
pastoral'. This closes the quartet and may be seen as the
true imaginative climax of the poem. The sestet, with its too-
much-discussed closing lines[1] represents Keats's final effort to
subdue his doubts about the urn. He had opened *Endymion*
with the line 'A thing of beauty is a joy for ever', a conception
now reintroduced with the urn, again humanized, as 'a

[1] For a summary of the principal arguments, see *The Poems of John Keats*,
ed. M. Allott, 1970, p. 537–8.

friend to man' who will console future generations 'in the midst of other woe than ours' with the one message it can offer. Its statement—

> 'Beauty is truth, truth beauty'—that is all
> Ye know on earth, and all ye need to know   (49–50)

—may be right or wrong. Keats does not say. It is the urn's offering and his decision to close with it brings a moment of repose.

There is a correspondence with these themes and ideas in the 'Ode on Melancholy', where the references to spring and early summer in the second of its three stanzas suggest that it too was written in May. The poem is perhaps the most concentrated expression of Keats's belief in the necessary relationship between joy and sorrow.

> Welcome joy and welcome sorrow,
>   Lethe's weed and Hermes' feather;
> Come today and come tomorrow,
>   I do love you both together!

are the opening lines of his 'little song' written in October 1818. Earlier he had described his 'pleasure-thermometer' in *Endymion*, Book I, as 'a first step' to his central theme, that is, 'the playing of different Natures with Joy and Sorrow', and had linked his 'Ode to Sorrow' in Book IV with his 'favourite Speculation', set out in a letter of November 1817 to his friend Benjamin Bailey: 'I am certain of nothing but of the holiness of the Heart's affections and the truth of Imagination —What the Imagination seizes as beauty must be truth . . . our Passions . . . are all in their sublime, creative of essential Beauty.' His youthful ode is attributed to the forlorn Indian maid. The burden of her song is

> Come then, Sorrow!
> Sweetest Sorrow!
> Like an own babe I nurse thee on my breast.
>   I thought to leave thee
>   And deceive thee,
> But now of all the world I love thee best   (IV, 279–84)

and it foreshadows his 1819 ode in connecting melancholy

with the perception of beauty a
nothing of the later poem's ric
repeat an earlier summary of m
runs, 'Melancholy is not to b
oblivion (stanza 1); it descends
beauty and its transience (sta
beauty, joy, pleasure and deligh
can experience these intensely
possess an imaginative consi
clear' after Keats had cancelle
first stanza with its macabre a

> Though you should buil
> And rear a phantom gibb
> Stitch creeds together fo
> To fill it out, blood-stain

the climax then being that o

> To find the Melancholy
> Dreameth in any isle of

The finished poem picks u

> No, no, go not to Leth
> Wolf's-bane, tight-roc

and thereafter unfolds ima
Keats's May 1819 self-con
moth as a 'mournful Psycl
resemble a human skull, a
was frequently represen
drugged relief of oblivic
drowsily/And drown the
because, as he finds in th
if it is awareness of pain,
is more, the 'wakeful ar
just as the 'weeping clc
droop-headed flowers
intense pleasure and ir
Turning to poison wl

[1] See *The Poems of John K*

finally
seeks t
its ow
where,
Endym
sexual i
betwee

A

As anot

His

indicates
(marked

Wh
Lov
Sou
Too
For

and the
elements
familiar f
in other p
sensation
climactic,
moods of
It is the
on Indole
fident orde
ence to a m
difficulty e

[1] Douglas I

individual stanzas, which differs in the various manuscripts. Understandably he omitted the ode from his 1820 collection, though he wrote to a friend in the June, 'You will judge of my 1819 temper when I tell you that the thing I have most enjoyed this year has been writing an ode to Indolence'. Whatever its weaknesses, its first inception represented a stage in the process leading to the 'Ode on the Grecian Urn'. On 19 March in a journal-letter Keats had written, 'This morning I am in a sort of temper indolent and supremely careless. . . . Neither Poetry, nor Ambition, nor Love have any alertness of countenance as they pass by me; they seem rather like three figures on a greek vase—a Man and two women. . . . This is the only happiness.' He must have begun the poem some time after re-reading this passage before sending the letter off in May (its closing entry is 3 May); there are throughout references to summer warmth, and the adoption of his special ode stanza suggests that it followed the 'Ode to a Nightingale' and the 'Ode on a Grecian Urn'. The theme runs alongside certain ideas belonging to the 'half' of Wordsworth which he said he greatly admired (the other 'half' he connected with Wordsworth's 'egotistical sublime'—at the opposite pole to Shakespearian 'Negative Capability'—and with the 'palpable design' of his explicit didacticism). His earlier unrhymed sonnet to the song of the thrush (of February 1819), 'O thou whose face has felt the winter's wind . . .', restates in his own terms the Wordsworthian theme of 'wise passiveness', especially as this is expressed in 'Expostulation and Reply' (1798),

> Books! 'tis a dull and endless strife:
> Come hear the woodland linnet,

and

> how blithe the throstle sings!
> He, too, is no mean preacher:
> Come forth into the life of things,
> Let Nature be your teacher.

Keats's thrush sings,

Oh, fret not after knowledge—I have none,
    And yet my song comes native with the warmth.
Oh, fret not after knowledge—I have none,
    And yet the evening listens.

His ode is less serene. It captures fleetingly the mood of deep passivity in the summer heat,

Ripe was the drowsy hour;
The blissful cloud of summer indolence
Benumbed my eyes; my pulse grew less and less;
Pain had no sting, and pleasure's wreath no flower   (15–18)

and turns away from the imaginatively quickening delight aroused by the display of energetic feeling celebrated in the 'Ode on Melancholy',

glut thy sorrow on a morning rose,
Or on the rainbow of the salt sand-wave,
Or on the wealth of globèd peonies;
Or if thy mistress some rich anger shows,
Imprison her soft hand, and let her rave,
And feed deep, deep upon her peerless eyes.   (15–20)

As the 'three figures' pass again before him (one guesses that some time has elapsed between the writing of one part of the poem and another),

like figures on a marble urn,
When shifted round to see the other side   (5–6)

he remains, it seems, unmoved.

The morn was clouded, but no shower fell,
Though in her lids hung the sweet tears of May;
The open casement pressed a new-leaved vine,
Let in the budding warmth and throstle's lay . . .

So ye three Ghosts, adieu! Ye cannot raise
My head cool-bedded in the flowery grass.
                                            (45–8; 51–2)

A belying want of ease nevertheless weakens the rest of the closing stanza, which falls into the irritable manner which often accompanies Keats's attempts at satirical humour:

For I would not be dieted with praise,
A pet-lamb in a sentimental farce!   (53–4)

Other instances of stylistic clumsiness affect his discourse
about his three visitants—

Oh, why did ye not melt, and leave my sense
Unhaunted quite of all but—nothingness?   (19–20)

—and it becomes increasingly plain that a certain bravado
mars his 'wise passiveness',

. . . to follow them I burned
And ached for wings because I knew the three;
The first was a fair maid, and Love her name;
The second was Ambition, pale of cheek,
And ever watchful with fatiguèd eye;
The last, whom I love more, the more of blame
Is heaped upon her, maiden most unmeek,
I knew to be my demon Poesy.   (23–30)

Like the other odes, this one draws on, even if it cannot
organize as they do, the feelings generated by Keats's major
1819 concerns. It assembles what are in effect a series of direct
personal statements and so sheds some light on important
fluctuations of feeling in his '1819 temper'. Its pretensions to
detachment present a remarkable contrast with his movement
in 'To Autumn' towards an unprecedently calm acceptance
of 'the object as in itself it is'. He wrote this ode in Winchester
on about 19 September, when he had not yet returned to
London and to Fanny, and was enjoying a brief mood of
quietude and self-containment. 'I "kepen in solitarinesse"',
he said peacefully, quoting his own 'imitation of the authors
in Chaucer's time' from 'The Eve of St Mark'. The weather
was mild and tranquillizing. 'How beautiful the season is
now,' he wrote to Reynolds, 'How fine the air. A temperate
sharpness about it. Really, without joking, chaste weather—
Dian skies—I never lik'd stubble fields so much as now—Aye
better than the chilly green of the spring. Somehow a stubble
plain looks warm . . . this struck me so much in my sunday's
walk that I composed upon it.' There is no flight from and
return to actuality as in the spring odes, 'Where are the songs
of Spring', he asks, 'Aye, where are they?' and answers,

'Think not of them, thou has thy music too.' He replaces the images of renewal and growth drawn on for the 'Ode to a Nightingale' by images of fullness and completion, for it seems now that 'ripeness is all'. Autumn is in league with the sun,

> To bend with apples the mossed cottage-trees,
>   And fill all fruit with ripeness to the core;
>   To swell the gourd, and plump the hazel shells
>   With a sweet kernel; to set budding more,
> And still more, later flowers for the bees.   (5–9)

But the poem depends for its unusual poise on exactly that sense of process and the movements of time which accompanied the evocation of summer in the 'Ode to a Nightingale' and which is found at work in all Keats's major poetry. The difference lies in the manner in which it is now brought under command. Keats had reached a moment of stillness at the close of his debate about the Grecian Urn by reproducing, with a strong desire to suspend disbelief, what he took to be its individual message of consolation and reassurance. In this poem he celebrates the period of time which lies between high summer and the onset of winter, as Collins in his 'Ode to Evening' celebrates the period which lies between day and night. For both poets, their subject subsumes ideas of process and change, while saluting a point of repose within that process. In Keats, the balanced, but still contrary, aspects of his chosen time are felt from the beginning, for this is a season of 'mists' as well as 'mellow fruitfulness', and throughout the poem words which suggest fullness also convey heaviness and the hint of decay. Summer has 'o'erbrimmed' the 'clammy cells' of the bees. Autumn, personified in the second stanza, watches 'the last oozings' of the cyder-press and, in the guise of a reaper, 'Spares the next swath and all its twinèd flowers', so that one senses along with munificence the scythe's ineluctable destructiveness (for if Autumn is a reaper, so is Time). The third stanza has the line, 'in a wailful choir the small gnats mourn', whose touchingly vivid visual and auditory effect owes much to the thought that the gnats are lamenting the shortness of their life and the lateness of the season. As one critic has put it, 'The music of Autumn which ends the poem is a music of living and dying, of staying and departure, of summer–winter'.[1]

The poem's success lies in its equipollent balancing of the contraries. The passage,

> And sometimes like a gleaner thou dost keep
> Steady thy laden head across a brook,

forms part of Keats's address to Autumn at the end of his second stanza, and the subject with the subtle metrical movement of the lines could be taken as a figure for his own poetic control. Leavis admired them because 'In the step from the rime-word "keep", across . . . the pause enforced by the line-division to "Steady", the balancing movement of the gleaner is enacted.' Douglas Bush, also testifying to the poem's metrical and structural skills, has spoken of the ordered deploying through the three stanzas of Keats's sense-responses to the season's ripeness and fulfilment: 'In the first stanza the sense of fullness and heaviness is given through mainly tactile images; in the second they are mainly visual . . . in the last the images are chiefly auditory'. It should be added that in this, the last and for many readers the finest, of his 1819 odes, Keats worked further on his own metrical innovations, adding an extra line to his ten-line stanza. This gave him still ampler room to 'load every rift with ore' at the same time that it imposed an additional discipline in its demand for another rhyming line.

For all this, I do not think we can say that 'To Autumn' represents a decisive new turn in Keats's artistic development. Rather, it seems to enact through its subject and style just such a moment of pause and equilibrium in his '1819 temper' as the tranquillizing season he celebrates may introduce into the cycle of the natural year. For a hint of the direction his genius might have taken we need to look, if anywhere, at the successive stages of his work on *Hyperion*.

[1] Arnold Davenport, 'A Note on "To Autumn" ', in *John Keats: A Reassessment*, ed. K. Muir, 1958, p. 98.

V. THE TWO *HYPERIONS*

These incomplete poems belong to a different and weightier order of achievement than the rest of Keats's poetry. If we take into account their germination, planning, composition and reconstruction, they can be said to span his entire poetic career from his first 'Ode to Apollo' in February 1815 to his final reworkings in December 1819, after which he wrote little more poetry of any significance. His first recorded references in 1817 are associated with Endymion, who is united with the goddess of the moon, sister to Apollo, the god of the sun, healing and, above all, music and poetry. 'Thy lute-voiced brother will I sing ere long' Keats tells his hero (*Endymion*, IV, 774) and refers in his 1818 preface to 'the beautiful mythology of Greece', which he wished 'to try once more, before I bid it farewell'. The projected poem had its title by 23 January 1818, when he advised Haydon, who wanted to use a passage from *Endymion* to illustrate a frontis-piece, 'wait for . . . *Hyperion* . . . the nature of *Hyperion* will lead me to treat it in a more naked and grecian Manner . . . the march of passion and endeavour will be undeviating . . . Apollo in *Hyperion* being a fore-seeing god will shape his actions like one'. He began composition in the autumn, but the juxtaposing of the two names shows that his subject matter was already established as the defeat of the Titans by the new race of Olympian gods, with the old and the new gods of the sun as the figures centrally opposed. The law of progress affirmed by Oceanus in the poem,

> 'tis the eternal law
> That first in beauty should be first in might   (II, 228–9)

and the identity of 'beauty' with wisdom and knowledge through suffering, by which Apollo is transfigured and im-mortalized, continue the arguments about individual development explored in 'Sleep and Poetry' and in Keats's May 1818 letter to Reynolds. This presents life as a 'Mansion of Many Apartments', beginning with 'the infant or thought-less Chamber' and going on to the 'Chamber of Maiden-Thought' which at first is filled with 'pleasant wonders' but is 'gradually darken'd' as we come to understand 'the heart and nature of Man' and the world as a place filled with 'Misery and Heartbreak, Pain, Sickness and oppression . . .'. 'Knowledge enormous makes a God of me', says Apollo in the presence of Mnemosyne, who has deserted the Titans for his sake, '. . . agonies/Creations and destroyings all at once,

> Pour into the wide hollows of my brain,
> And deify me, as if some blithe wine
> Or bright elixir peerless I had drunk,
> And so become immortal.'   (III, 117–20)

Keats abandoned the first version of the poem at this climax in April 1819, and went on to write his shorter narratives, his experimental sonnets and the Spring odes. His reconstruction, which he worked at intermittently in the months from July to September and seemingly again in November to December, stops short at the entry of Apollo's predecessor Hyperion. Of the various reasons offered as an explanation for this second abandonment of the poem, the most important are connected with Keats's attempt to reconstruct it as a vision in which the defeat of the Titans is related by the priestess Moneta, an august reincarnation of Mnemosyne. The theme of suffering and its effect on the poetic imagination receives a stronger personal emphasis, with the poet assuming Apollo's role as he drinks the magical 'elixir' which induces his vision. It is central to the debate in the first canto, which turns on the general question of the poet's value to humanity and the particular question of Keats's poetic achievement. He is admitted to Moneta's shrine as one of those

> to whom the miseries of the world
> Are misery, and will not let them rest,   (I, 148–9)

but her stern lesson is that this is not enough.

> 'Art thou not of the dreamer tribe?
> The poet and the dreamer are distinct,
> Diverse, sheer opposite, antipodes.
> The one pours out a balm upon the world,
> The other vexes it.'   (I, 198–202)

41

The poet 'pours . . . balm' on suffering because of his knowledge and wisdom; the dreamer 'vexes' it, adding to its
troubles by dwelling on 'miseries' without suggesting how to
face them. On 21 September Keats told Reynolds that he had
given up the poem because 'there were too many Miltonic
inversions in it . . . Miltonic verse cannot be written but in an
artful or rather artist's humour . . . I wish to give myself up to
other sensations . . . English ought to be kept up'; the same
letter records his composition of 'To Autumn', his association
of Chatterton with the season, and his admiration of him as
'the purest poet in the English language'. But clearly there was
also the problem of sustaining his exploratory personal
statement at the same time as Moneta's 'seer's' vision of the
past. Above all, there was the intractable fact that in his
revised first canto—which takes its direction from the
original *Hyperion's* climatic third canto—he had already
given vivid dramatic expression to his central themes.

The evolution and expression of these themes in the two
versions reflects Keats's imaginative development, from the
youthful celebrant of 'poesy' in 'Sleep and Poetry' who
yearned to

> die a death
> Of luxury and my young spirit follow
> The morning sunbeams to the great Apollo
> Like a fresh sacrifice   (58–61)

to the poet acquainted with the 'sharp anguish' of death who
records in his vision of Moneta's unveiled face the mystery
and dignity of suffering:

> Then saw I a wan face,
> Not pined by human sorrows, but bright-blanched
> By an immortal sickness which kills not.
> It works a constant change, which happy death
> Can put no end to; deathwards progressing
> To no death was that visage; it had passed
> The lily and the snow; and beyond these
> I must not think now, though I saw that face—
>   (I, 256–63)

There are no 'Miltonic' inversions in this blank verse nor is it

42

ostensibly the work of an 'epic' poet, though in 1817 the writing of an epical poem would probably appear to be a natural sequel to the long trial-run in *Endymion*, which had given Keats practice in sustaining a narrative through which to dramatize ideas important to him. Further, in 1817 he had added to his renewed familiarity with Shakespeare by beginning to read Milton seriously for the first time. 'Shakespeare and the paradise Lost every day become greater wonders', he wrote in August 1819, adding a week or two later in a similar context, 'The more I know what my diligence may in time probably effect, the more does my heart distend with Pride and Obstinacy.' It was in the following month that he changed his mind—'I have but lately stood upon my guard against Milton. Life to him would be death to me'—and asked Reynolds to 'pick out some lines from *Hyperion* and put a mark X to the false beauty proceeding from art, and one || to the true voice of feeling'. That his instinct was true as usual to his current poetic needs is apparent from his handling of the new material in *The Fall of Hyperion*, but his former ardour accounts for strength as well as weakness. His Miltonic constructions are certainly intrusive— 'thunder . . . rumbles reluctant'; 'came slope upon the threshold of the west'; 'gold clouds metropolitan'; 'Regal his shape majestic'. Yet his 'stationing' of his figures owes much to the grouping which he praised in a marginal note to *Paradise Lost*, VII, 420–4, 'Milton . . . pursues his imagination to the utmost . . . in no instance . . . more exemplified than in his *stationing* or *statury*. He is not content with simple description, he must station . . .'. His own finest instance provides the first *Hyperion* with its impressive opening:

> Deep in the shady sadness of a vale
> Far sunken from the healthy breath of morn,
> Far from the fiery noon, and eve's one star,
> Sat grey-haired Saturn, quiet as a stone,
> Still as the silence round about his lair.

Keats's disposition of the other fallen Titans, situated amid cavernous rocks and 'the solid roar/Of thunderous waterfalls and torrents hoarse' in attitudes of anger, grief and despair, aims, though not with consistent success, for a similar effect, and their ensuing debate obviously derives from the 'Stygian council' in Milton's Pandemonium. But inspiration is not imitation and Keats's poem takes its own course. As always in his work, it is nourished by a wide range of literary and personal experiences. Some of the 'Miltonic' grandeur is in fact owed to his enthusiastic response to the scenery in the Lakes and Scotland during his summer walking tour. He wrote then a number of slight poems but many lengthy vivid letters, among them a description for Tom of Fingal's Cave, which he called 'this cathedral of the sea'—'suppose the Giants who rebelled against Jove had taken a whole Mass of black Columns and bound them together like bundles of matches—and then with immense Axes had made a cavern in the body of these columns'—and which he remembered later in his 'stationing' of Saturn and Thea,

> these two were pictured motionless,
> Like natural sculpture in cathedral cavern.   (I, 85–6)

Keats's reading on the tour was confined to the 1814 edition of Dante's *Divina Commedia* which added its own contribution to the solemnity of the first *Hyperion* and was instrumental in shaping the second, for it stimulated Keats's eager study during the following summer of the original Italian, especially, to judge by the cadences and echoes in *The Fall of Hyperion*, the *Purgatorio*, which certainly affected his own purgatorial 'vision' and gave his portrayal of Moneta some flavour of the mingled awe and benignity surrounding Dante's Beatrice.

The 'shaping force' at work upon these diverse elements is still unequal to a sustained flight, and is at its most disappointing in handling the pivotal theme. The Titans are men of power and identity; their successors, the Olympians, whose qualities are epitomized in Apollo, have no identity and represent Keats's idea of the poetical character as he expressed it in a letter of 27 October 1818, '... the poetical Character ... that sort distinguished from the wordsworthian or egotistical sublime ... is not itself—it has no self ... A poet ... has no character ... A poet has no Identity—he is continually ... filling some other body'. He had written the previous November, 'Men of Genius are great as certain etherial

Chemicals operating on the Mass of neutral intellect . . . they have not any individuality, any determined Character. I would call the top and head of those who have a proper self Men of Power.' He knew from his classical reading that although Hyperion preceded Apollo as god of the sun he was endowed with no power over music and poetry. In the first *Hyperion*, although he makes his Titan less consistently magnificent than the gorgeous palace which he inhabits (it takes some hints from Wordsworth's cloud palace in *The Excursion*, II, 839–40, and the halls of Eblis in Beckford's *Vathek*), he succeeds nevertheless in making him unmistakably a 'Man of Power'.

> He entered, but he entered full of wrath;
> His flaming robes streamed out beyond his heels,
> And gave a roar . . .
>   On he flared,
> From stately nave to nave, from vault to vault,
>   (I, 213–18)

and his self-centred rage is the expression of his threatened 'identity':

> '. . . Why
> Is my eternal essence thus distraught
> To see and behold these horrors new?
> Saturn is fallen, am I too to fall?
> Am I to leave this haven of my rest,
> This cradle of my glory . . .'   (I, 231–6)

This invests the figure with at least sufficiently appropriate poetic force, but on the entry of Apollo in canto III Keats reverts disastrously to the fruity manner of his *Endymion*. Apollo, deified by 'knowledge enormous' of the world's suffering and supposedly endowed with the imaginative power dependent on such knowledge, remains an effeminate figure, who 'weeps and wonders somewhat too fondly', as Leigh Hunt said in 1820, though Hunt also thought that 'his powers gather nobly on him as he proceeds'. The 'nobility' belongs, in truth, only to the few lines, quoted earlier, which record the accession of his visionary insight. The poem closes with the semi-erotic description,

Soon wild commotions shook him, and made flush
All the immortal fairness of his limbs . . .
                    So young Apollo anguished;
His very hair, his golden tresses famed,
Kept undulation round his eager neck.

                                   (III, 124–5; 130–2)

Mnemosyne the while holds up her arms 'as one who prophesied', and

                        At length
Apollo shrieked—and lo! from all his limbs
Celestial . . .   (III, 134–6)

And there it ends, with the poet seemingly (and under-standably) stumped and the entire war of the Titans against the Olympians yet to record. A year later Keats had trans-formed this material into the intensely imaginative personal statement of the first canto of *The Fall of Hyperion*.

If we try to hold the two versions together in our mind as one poem, it is apparent at once that they represent two totally different kinds of poetic impulse. Keats's themes and his creative temper in any case could never have lent themselves fully to expression through an epic conflict in the high Miltonic style which he had tried for in his first version. He makes, it is true, a valiant, and far from unsuccessful, effort to dramatize his ideas about suffering and creativity in his Titans, especially when he differentiates between the grief of the fallen Saturn and Thea, whom sorrow has made 'more beautiful than Beauty's self', the rage of 'huge Enceladus', whose words boom among his fellows,

                              like sullen waves
In the half-glutted hollows of reef-rocks,   (II, 305–6)

and the different kind of pain felt by the stoical Oceanus, who understands the law by which he must perish, and the simpler Clymene, who alone has heard the song of Apollo, felt the 'living death' of its melody and knows what it is to be,

                        sick
Of joy and grief at once.   (II, 288–9)

But his recasting of the material for *The Fall of Hyperion*, whatever the rights and wrongs of moving from a more 'objective' to a more 'subjective' kind of writing, is entirely consistent with two strong impulses seen at work in his poetry from the beginning. There is the direct confessional impulse, which found early expression in 'Sleep and Poetry', and there is the impulse towards a more oblique expression of important personal themes which shapes in some degree all the narrative poems and the major odes. Looked at in this way, *The Fall of Hyperion* with its mixture of earnestness about the importance of the poet's 'public' role, its jealous feeling nevertheless for the poet's individual voice, and its projection of personal themes through a fictional situation, is not only seen to build on these impulses but also offers an early example of the tendency towards the fictionalized spiritual autobiography which is so common in Victorian prose and poetry. Carlyle, we said, was born in the same year as Keats, and his *Sartor Resartus* is often regarded as the first major example of the Victorian habit of disguising as a fiction the history of pressing inner conflict. Other examples, dealing especially with the role of the creative writer in his struggle to penetrate the romantic dream, run from 'The Lady of Shalott' to 'Empedocles on Etna'. It could be said that all these have an early precursor in *The Fall of Hyperion*, and that Keats's 'vision' hints at a potential development of the youthful Romantic poet into a writer who might have been a particularly eminent Victorian.

VI. THE LETTERS

At about the time of his last attempts to rework *Hyperion*, Keats wrote to his publisher John Taylor, on 17 November 1819,

I have come to a determination not to publish any thing I have now ready written; but for all that to publish a Poem before long and that I hope to make a fine one. As the marvellous is the most enticing and the surest guarantee of harmonious numbers I have been endeavouring to persuade myself to untether Fancy and let her manage for herself—I and myself cannot agree about this at all. Wonders are no wonders to me. I am more at home amongst Men and women. I would rather read Chaucer than Ariosto—The little dramatic skill I may as yet have however badly it might show in a Drama would I think be sufficient for a Poem—I wish to diffuse the colouring of St Agnes eve throughout a Poem in which Character and Sentiment would be the figures to such drapery— Two or three such Poems, if God should spare me, written in the course of the next six years, would be a famous *gradus ad Parnassum altissimum* . . . they would nerve me up to the writing of a few fine Plays—my greatest ambition—when I do feel ambitious.

This is one of the last major statements about his poetic intentions in Keats's letters and it demonstrates the shrewdness of his self-knowledge and the consistency of his debate with himself about his poetry since at least late 1816. Behind his wide range of poetic experimentalism is the unchanging impulse to overcome his native longing for an ideal 'romantic' world, in order to reach a Shakespearian understanding and acceptance of the world as it is. A few months before his letter to Taylor, in June 1819, he had distinguished Matteo Boiardo from Shakespeare, as 'a noble Poet of Romance; not a miserable and mighty Poet of the human Heart'. His gifts, at the stage we see them, and particularly in his narratives, where he tries to present the passions of 'men and women', are plainly not in keeping with his ambitions. We find him less the 'Poet of the human heart' that he wished to be than the poet of the 'wonders' which he wanted to grow away from. It is hardly surprising that his one play, the melodramatic *Otho the Great*, written in collaboration with Charles Brown and worked on in the months when he was composing 'Lamia' and revising *Hyperion*, is not 'fine' at all; nor that the quality of the fragmentary *King Stephen* of the same period, which was also designed as a vehicle for his admired Edmund Kean, rests exclusively on its few but by no means unimpressive passages of quasi-Shakespearian blank verse. As a writer of prose, on the other hand, Keats is often several jumps ahead of his poetic practice. His letters are perhaps the most vivacious expression of lively and unpretending intelligence in English literary history (there is no eye to posterity in them). They mirror from day to day and sometimes from hour to hour, the rapid movements of his thinking and feeling, his excited gaiety in observing the world around him and his remarkably knowledgeable, sensitive and unselfregarding feeling for other people. Few literary figures, few people anywhere, have won so much affection and respect from their associates. Many of his circle, prominently Charles Brown, John Hamilton Reynolds and Richard Woodhouse, are known to posterity primarily because of his correspondence with them and their own care in preserving copies of his letters and poems (this is one reason why there is such a wealth of Keatsian manuscript material in existence). Characteristically, once his brother George had left for America in June 1818 with his wife Georgiana, Keats took pains to write long, affectionate newsy journal-letters, recording daily happenings and copying out with comments many of his recent poems. So his letters provide a magnificent gloss on his poetry and they also help to explain why he has been so fortunate in his modern biographers, who since 1958 have been able to consult them in Hyder Rollins's superb annotated edition. They form, in effect, an integral part of his creative life and should be required reading for anyone interested in literature, in particular poetry, the poetic process and the nature of poetic sensibility. If there is immaturity in their volatile expression and flexibility,[1] there is also unusual self-knowledge. Keats had no doubts about his ultimate goal, only about how to reach it, and recognized that in exploring possibilities he would swing between opposite poles and 'take but three steps from feathers to iron'. He used this sharp image on 13 March 1818 to Benjamin Bailey, after copying his sonnet, 'Four seasons fill the measure of the year . . .', which foreshadows the balanced mood but not the imaginative poise of 'To Autumn'. The relaxed informal prose of his accompanying remarks, with their darting parentheses and sudden flashes of insight, enacts the ebb and flow of his 'speculations'. 'I shall never be a reasoner because I do not care to be in the right',

[1] And also, one should add, in their engagingly idiosyncratic spelling and punctuation.

he declares, and persuades his reader through the suggestive-
ness rather than the logic of his improvisations on the theme
that 'every mental pursuit takes its reality and worth from the
ardour of the pursuer—being in itself a nothing'. There are

Things real—such as existences of Sun Moon & Stars and passages
of Shakspeare—Things semireal such as Love, the Clouds &c
which require a greeting of the Spirit to make them wholly
exist—and Nothings which are made Great and dignified by an
ardent pursuit . . .

Even 'poetry itself', in his 'very sceptical' moods, may appear
'a mere Jack a lantern to amuse anyone who may be struck
with its brilliance'.

   This letter clearly represents a stage in the continued com-
munings with himself and his friends which carried him from
his ideas about 'Negative Capability' at the end of 1817 to
his definition in October 1818 of the 'poetical character' and
his poignant affirmation of his dramatic ambitions in November 1819. As he walked away from a Christmas pantomime
in December 1817 he was caught up in 'a disquisition with
[Charles] Dilke' and 'several things dovetailed in my mind':

at once it struck me, what quality went to form a Man of Achievement especially in Literature & which Shakespeare posessed so
enormously—I mean *Negative Capability*, that is when man is
capable of being in uncertainties, Mysteries, doubts, without any
irritable reaching after fact & reason.

A day or two earlier, while admiring a painting by Nathaniel
West, he had nevertheless missed in it 'the excellence of every
Art', which lies 'in its intensity, capable of making all disa-
greeables evaporate, from being in close relationship with
Beauty and Truth—examine King Lear and you will find
this examplified [*sic*] throughout'. He closes his 'Negative
Capability' passage with the reflection that he is saying no
more than that 'with a great poet the sense of Beauty over-
comes every other consideration'. A year later his description
of 'the poetical character' once more emphasizes his openness
of response and refusal to tie himself to unexamined axio-
matic systems ('axioms in philosophy are not axioms until
they are proved on our pulses', he explains in his May 1818

letter to John Reynolds). He is not concerned, he says, with 'the wordsworthian or egotistical sublime . . . a thing *per se*', for which he felt mingled admiration and distaste. 'We hate poetry that has a palpable design upon us', he said in February 1818 when thinking of Wordsworth's 'bullying' didacticism, 'Poetry should be great and unobtrusive'; yet he was deeply indebted to this elder statesman among contemporary poets and in the previous month had praised *The Excursion* as one of the few artistic achievements 'to rejoice at in this Age'. The 'poetical character' with which he identifies himself,

has no self—it is every thing and nothing—It has no character—it enjoys light and shade; it lives in gusto, be it foul or fair, high or low, rich or poor, mean or elevated—It has as much delight in conceiving an Iago as an Imogen. What shocks the virtuous philosop[h]er, delights the camelion Poet . . . A Poet is the most unpoetical of any thing in existence; because he has no Identity— he is continually . . . filling some other Body.

The ability to recreate his own experience of 'filling some other body' is at best fitful in his poems, but the experience itself is constantly displayed in his letters. He is aware of it when he speaks of being 'annihilated' when in a room full of other 'identities', of being 'pressed' upon by the identity of Tom or his sister Fanny, and 'if a Sparrow came before my Window I take part in his existence and pick about the Gravel'. Similarly, he responds instinctively to the individual temper of his correspondents. Bailey, the friend who studied theology and took orders, prompted his discussion in November 1817, quoted earlier in this essay, about the relative value of 'consequitive thinking' and 'sensations' as a means of penetrating truth, and led him on to his celebrated reflections about a possible after life, where perhaps 'we shall enjoy ourselves . . . by having what we called happiness on earth repeated in a finer tone'. His letters to Reynolds, in-cluding the verse epistle written in March 1818 to cheer him when ill, are stimulated by his responsiveness to this close friend's own interests in writing poetry and read like con-tinuations of their conversations together. His analysis of life as a 'Mansion of Many Apartments' is designed to draw

Reynolds into its reassuring arguments about the uncertainties of youthful years—'We see not the ballance of good and evil. We are in a Mist—We are now in that state—We feel the "burden of the Mystery", To this point was Wordsworth come . . . when he wrote "Tintern Abbey" and . . . his Genius is explorative of those dark Passages. Now if we live, and go on thinking, we too shall explore them . . .'. It was Reynolds, as we saw, whom he asked to distinguish the Miltonisms from 'the true voice of feeling' in *Hyperion*. To John Taylor, his publisher, and Richard Woodhouse, the lawyer who faithfully transcribed numerous letters and poems and sometimes acted as an intermediary with his publishers, he writes, so to speak, more 'publicly' and informatively about his artistic progress, setting out for Taylor in March 1818, as a kind of apologia, 'axioms' about poetry which he thinks *Endymion* has not met ('Poetry should surprise by a fine excess . . . Its touches of beauty should never be half way . . . If Poetry comes not as naturally as leaves to a tree it had better not come at all . . .'). He adapts himself quite differently to the Reynolds sisters, whom he quizzes inventively while staying with Bailey at Oxford in September 1817, '. . . here am I among Colleges, Halls, Stalls . . . but you are by the sea . . . argal you bathe—you walk—you say how beautiful—find out resemblances between waves and Camels—rocks and dancing Masters—fireshovels and telescopes—Dolphins and Madonas . . .'. He writes for his brothers vigorously raffish Regency jokes about his dancing and drinking parties in late 1817 and early 1818, when he was released from his dogged labours on *Endymion* and for a short time could indulge his pleasure in company and his liking for claret; cracks awful puns for them and for Charles Brown, who was waggish in this way and encouraged such jokes (not very happily for his poetry) when Keats was walking with him in Scotland and living with him at Hampstead after Tom's death; and he invents amusing fantasies to entertain his young sister Fanny. For his brothers, again, he particularizes the magnificences of the waterfalls, the changing colours of slate and stone, and the mixed exhilaration and discomfort of climbing the vast heights of Ailsa Craig and Ben Nevis during his walking tour with Brown.

This quickness of sensibility made it impossible for him to respond to experience or to compose poetry tranquilly. The word 'fever' recurs in his accounts of his active creative moods, which were usually preceded and followed by the 'indolence' which he celebrates in his 1819 ode ('Thou art a fever of thyself', is Moneta's scathing reproach in *The Fall of Hyperion*). It appears in another context when finally, in late 1819, he begins to speak, circuitously, about his current feeling for women. A beautiful woman, he tells George and Georgiana Keats, can haunt him 'as a tune of Mozart's might do' and if she distracts him from poetry, 'that is a fever'. About his feelings for Fanny Brawne he was deeply reticent to everyone except herself. His letters to her worried Matthew Arnold, who thought them effeminate (this was the later, settled, Arnold, who long ago had made his own troubled accommodations about his feelings for Marguerite). But in the context of everything we know about Keats, these love letters, with the generosity of their total emotional commitment, are exactly what we should expect from him. They are at first passionate, tender and amusingly inventive. Later, when he was torn apart first by fears for his imaginative freedom and afterwards by his appalling despair at having been separated from her through illness and the tragically ill-advised journey to Italy, they become the most ravaging of any personal letters to have appeared in print.

We see everywhere in all these extraordinarily attaching human documents the play of a particular kind of creative sensibility which vitalizes everything which it contemplates, and does so by the peculiar immediacy with which it simultaneously senses and reflects upon the objects of its experience. Long before T. S. Eliot's remarks about the 'dissociation of sensibility', Arthur Hallam, the subject of Tennyson's *In Memoriam* and himself a young poet (he died at twenty-two), saluted in a brilliant article of 1831 the interplay of 'sensation' and 'thought' in certain modern poets, notably Keats and Shelley. 'The tenderness of Keats', he says, 'cannot sustain a lofty flight' and like Shelley he is a poet 'of sensation'. Yet 'so vivid was the delight attending the simple exertions of eye and ear, that it became mingled more and more with their trains of active thought, and tended to absorb their whole being in the energy of sense'. Had he lived long enough to read more of Keats's letters in Milnes's 1848 edition of the *Life, Letters and Literary Remains*, and also *The Fall of Hyperion* when it appeared a few years later, he would probably have emphasized even more strongly the 'reflective' components contributing to that 'energy of sense' in Keats. Eliot saw 'traces of a struggle towards unification of sensibility' in the second *Hyperion*. We could add that there is evidence of such a struggle from the beginning and that Keats in his letters provides a conscious and continuous commentary upon it.

JOHN KEATS

A Select Bibliography

(Place of publication London, unless stated otherwise. Detailed bibliographical information will also be found in the appropriate volumes of *The New Cambridge Bibliography of English Literature* and *The Oxford History of English Literature*. See also the *Keats–Shelley Journal*, which carries annual bibliographies; for its bibliographies to June 1962, see below).

Bibliography:

CATALOGUE OF A LOAN EXHIBITION Commemorating the Anniversary of the Death of John Keats (1821–1921) held at the Public Library, Boston, February 21–March 14, 1921.

THE JOHN KEATS MEMORIAL VOLUME (1921)
—contains 'A Bibliography of the Writings of John Keats', by T. J. Wise.

THE ASHLEY LIBRARY: A Catalogue of Printed Books, Manuscripts and Letters, collected by T. J. Wise (1928)
—printed for private circulation. Contains a description of books and MSS by or relating to Keats.

KEATS: A Bibliography and Reference Guide, with an Essay on Keats' reputation, by J. R. Macgillivray (1949).

KEATS, SHELLEY, BYRON, HUNT AND THEIR CIRCLES: Bibliographies from the *Keats–Shelley Journal*, July 1, 1950–June 30, 1962, ed. D. Bonnell Green and E. G. Wilson; Nebraska, 1964.

Collected Editions:

THE POETICAL WORKS OF COLERIDGE, SHELLEY AND KEATS; Paris (1829)
—the Galignani edition.

THE POETICAL WORKS (1840)
—in Smith's Standard Library. The first English collected edition.

THE POETICAL WORKS. With a Memoir by R. M. Milnes [Lord Houghton] (1854)
—the first illustrated edition, with 120 designs by George Scharf.

THE POETICAL WORKS, edited with a Critical Memoir by W. M. Rossetti (1872).

THE POETICAL WORKS, ed. Lord Houghton [R. M. Milnes] (1876)
—the Aldine Edition.

THE POETICAL WORKS AND OTHER WRITINGS, ed. H. Buxton Forman, 4 vols (1883)
—Vols. III and IV contain Keats's letters.

THE POEMS, ed. G. Thorn-Drury. With an introduction by R. Bridges, 2 vols (1896).

THE COMPLETE POETICAL WORKS AND LETTERS, ed. H. E. Scudder; Boston & New York (1899)
—the Cambridge Edition.

THE COMPLETE WORKS, ed. H. Buxton Forman, 5 vols; Glasgow (1900–1)
—brings the editions of 1883 and 1889 up to date with new material and biographical notes.

THE POEMS, ed. E. de Sélincourt (1905)
—with introduction and notes. Revised editions, 1907 and 1926.

THE POETICAL WORKS, ed. H. Buxton Forman (1906). With Introduction and textual notes, ed. H. W. Garrod, 1956.

POEMS OF JOHN KEATS, ed. and arranged in chronological order by J. M. Murry (1930).

POETICAL WORKS, ed. H. W. Garrod (1939)
—the Oxford Variorum edition, revised 1958.

THE POEMS OF JOHN KEATS, ed. Miriam Allott (1970)
—the first complete, chronological, annotated edition. Reprinted with revisions, London and New York, 1972; revised paperback edition, 1973.

JOHN KEATS: THE COMPLETE POEMS, ed. John Barnard (1973)
—useful, inexpensive annotated edition, with poems printed in chronological order.

Selected Works:

LIFE, LETTERS AND LITERARY REMAINS OF JOHN KEATS, ed. R. M. Milnes [Lord Houghton], 2 vols (1848)
—prints many poems and letters for the first time, including Keats's tragedy *Otho the Great*.

THE EVE OF ST AGNES, AND OTHER POEMS; Boston (1876)
—part of the 'Vest-Pocket' Series of Standard and Popular Authors.

ODES AND SONNETS; Philadelphia (1888)
—with illustrative designs by W. H. Low.

SELECTIONS FROM KEATS (1889)
—with a preface by J. R. Tutin. Includes all the poems from the 1820 volume and a selection from the other.

THE ODES OF KEATS, with Notes and Analyses and a Memoir by A. C. Downer; Oxford (1897)
—facsimile of 1897 edition, Tokyo, 1965.

ENDYMION AND THE LONGER POEMS, ed. H. Buxton Forman (1897).

POETRY AND PROSE, ed. H. Ellershaw; Oxford (1922)
—with essays by Lamb, Leigh Hunt, Bridges, and others.

POEMS. With Selections from his Letters and from Criticism, ed. C. W. Thomas (1932)
—includes criticism by de Sélincourt, Bridges, Bradley.
SELECTED LETTERS AND POEMS, ed. J. A. Walsh (1954).
SELECTED POEMS, ed. E. C. Blunden (1955).
SELECTED POEMS AND LETTERS OF JOHN KEATS, ed. R. Gittings (1967).

Separate Works:

POEMS (1817)
—a facsimile of the 1817 edition in the Noel Douglas Replicas series, 1927.
ENDYMION: A Poetic romance (1818)
—a type-facsimile edition with introduction and notes by C. E. Notcutt, 1927. See also T. Saito's edition of *Endymion*, with notes, 1931.
LAMIA, ISABELLA, THE EVE OF ST AGNES, AND OTHER POEMS (1820)
—facsimile ed., 1970.
ANOTHER VERSION OF KEATS'S HYPERION [1857?]
—reprint of R. M. Milnes's contribution to the *Miscellanies of the Philobiblon Society*, III, 1856-7. The basic text of *The Fall of Hyperion: A Dream* until the discovery of the Woodhouse Transcript in 1904.
'La Belle Dame Sans Merci', *The Indicator*, 10 May, 1820
—the poem is signed 'Caviare'.
HYPERION. A Facsimile of Keats's Autograph Manuscript with a Transliteration of the Manuscript of *The Fall of Hyperion: A Dream*, with Introduction and Notes by E. de Sélincourt (1905).
THE ODES OF KEATS AND THEIR EARLIEST KNOWN MANUSCRIPTS, edited with introduction and notes by Robert Gittings (1970).
Note: Students should also consult *The Examiner*, *The Indicator*, *The Annals of the Fine Arts*, *Blackwood's Magazine* and other journals of Keats's day.

Letters:

LETTERS TO FANNY BRAWNE, 1819-1820. With Introduction and Notes by H. Buxton Forman (1878).
LETTERS, ed. J. G. Speed; New York (1883).
LETTERS TO HIS FAMILY AND FRIENDS, ed. S. Colvin (1891)
—excludes letters to Fanny Brawne.
LETTERS, ed. H. Buxton Forman (1895)
—contains every letter of Keats known at the time.
THE KEATS LETTERS, PAPERS AND OTHER RELICS FORMING THE DILKE BEQUEST, ed. T. Watts-Dunton, G. Williamson and H. Buxton Forman (1914).

LETTERS, ed. M. B. Forman, 2 vols (1931)
—the revised edition of 1935 adds ten further letters.
THE KEATS CIRCLE: Letters and papers, 1816–78, ed. Hyder Rollins. 2 vols; Cambridge, Mass. (1948).
MORE LETTERS AND POEMS OF THE KEATS CIRCLE, ed. Hyder Rollins; Cambridge, Mass. (1955)
—a new edition entitled *The Keats Circle: Letters and Papers and More Letters and Poems of the Keats Circle*, 1965, contains the 1948 and 1955 publications in 2 vols.
THE LETTERS OF JOHN KEATS, 1814–1821, ed. Hyder Rollins (1958)
—the definitive edition.
LETTERS OF JOHN KEATS, ed. R. Gittings (1970)
—replaces F. Page's selection in the World's Classics series.
Note: See also *Collected Editions, Selected Works* and *Some Biographical and Critical Studies.*

Some Biographical and Critical Studies:
ADONAIS: An Elegy on the death of John Keats, by P. B. Shelley (1821).
LORD BYRON AND SOME OF HIS CONTEMPORARIES, by L. Hunt (1828)
—contains an account of Keats with criticism of his poetry; ed. J. E. Morpurgo, 1949.
'On Some of the Characteristics of Modern Poetry', by Arthur Hallam, *Englishman's Magazine*, I, August 1831, 616–21
—discusses Tennyson, with arresting analysis of Keats as his forerunner. Reprinted in *The Critical Heritage*, ed. G. Matthews, 1971.
THE BOOK OF GEMS, Vol. III, ed. S. C. Hall (1838)
—contains comment on Keats by L. Hunt.
IMAGINATION AND FANCY, by L. Hunt (1844)
—ed. Sir E. Gosse, 1907.
THE LIFE OF PERCY BYSSHE SHELLEY, by T. Medwin, 2 vols (1847)
—contains comment on Keats, based on information from Leigh Hunt, Fanny Brawne and Shelley.
LIFE, LETTERS AND LITERARY REMAINS OF JOHN KEATS, ed. R. M. Milnes (1848). See under *Selected Works* above
—reviewed by Aubrey de Vere in *Edinburgh Review*, XC, October 1849, 388–433, in a perceptive essay comparing Keats, Shelley and Tennyson. Reprinted in *The Critical Heritage*, ed. G. Matthews, 1971.
POETICS: An Essay on poetry, by E. S. Dallas (1852).
LIFE OF B. R. HAYDON FROM HIS AUTOBIOGRAPHY AND JOURNALS, ed. T. Taylor, 3 vols (1853).
'The Life and Poetry of Keats', by David Masson, *Macmillan's Magazine*, November 1860, 1–16
—an important lengthy essay anticipating some aspects of modern

criticism of Keats. Reprinted in *The Critical Heritage*, ed. G. Matthews, 1971.

ON THE STUDY OF CELTIC LITERATURE, by M. Arnold (1867)
—chapter iv refers to Keats's 'natural magic'; see also M. Arnold's essay, 'Maurice et Guérin', in *Essays in Criticism*, 1865.

MY STUDY WINDOWS, ed. J. R. Lowell (1871)
—forming part of Low's American Copyright Series of American Authors.

THE PAPERS OF A CRITIC, by Sir C. W. Dilke, 2 vols (1875)
—the Memoir by Sir C. W. Dilke contains letters from Keats, etc.

RECOLLECTIONS OF WRITERS, by C. and M. Cowden Clarke (1878).

THE ENGLISH POETS: Selections, with a general introduction by M. Arnold, ed. T. H. Ward (1880)
—Vol IV contains essay on Keats by M. Arnold, republished in *Essays in Criticism*, 1888.

JOHN KEATS: A Study, by F. M. Owen (1880).

KEATS, by S. Colvin (1887)
—in the 'English Men of Letters' Series. New edition, 1889.

LIFE OF JOHN KEATS, by W. M. Rossetti (1887)
—contains a bibliography by J. P. Anderson.

THE LIFE AND LETTERS OF JOSEPH SEVERN, by W. Sharp (1892).

JOHN KEATS: A Critical essay, by R. Bridges (1895)
—privately printed; published in the Muses' Library, 1896. Republished in *Collected Essays*, IV, 1929.

The Bookman. Keats Double Number, October 1906
—contains original material relating to Keats.

OXFORD LECTURES ON POETRY, by A. C. Bradley (1909)
—contains an essay on 'The Letters of Keats' followed by a comparison of Keats's *Endymion* and Shelley's 'Alastor'. Reprinted with introduction by M. R. Ridley, 1965.

JOHN KEATS: Sa vie et son oeuvre, 1795–1821, by L. Wolff; Paris (1910).

KEATS, by E. Thomas (1916).

A CONCORDANCE TO THE POEMS OF JOHN KEATS, ed. D. L. Baldwin; Washington (1917).

JOHN KEATS: His life and poetry, his friends, critics and after-fame, by S. Colvin (1917).
—rev. edition, 1925.

JOHN KEATS MEMORIAL VOLUME, issued by Keats House Committee, Hampstead (1921).

KEATS: A Study in development, by H. I'A. Fausset (1922).

JOHN KEATS, by A. Lowell, 2 vols; Boston (1925).

KEATS AND SHAKESPEARE: A Study of Keats's poetic life from 1816 to 1820, by J. M. Murry (1925).

KEATS, by H. W. Garrod; Oxford (1926).

LEIGH HUNT'S EXAMINER EXAMINED, by E. Blunden (1928).

KEATS'S SHAKESPEARE: A Descriptive study, by C. Spurgeon (1928)
—based on Keats's markings and marginalia in his copies of Shakespeare.

JOHN HAMILTON REYNOLDS, POETRY AND PROSE, with an Introduction and Notes by G. L. Marsh (1928).

KEATS'S VIEW OF POETRY, by T. Saito (1929).

KEATS, by L. Wolff; Paris (1929).

STUDIES IN KEATS, by J. M. Murry (1930)
—revised and enlarged as *Studies in Keats, New and Old*, 1939, as *The Mystery of Keats*, 1949, and as *Keats*, 1955.

KEATS'S CRAFTMANSHIP: A Study in poetic development, by M. R. Ridley; Oxford (1933).

KEATS HOUSE AND MUSEUM: An Historical and descriptive guide (1934)
—new edition 1966; 7th ed., 1974.

KEATS'S PUBLISHER: A Memoir of John Taylor, by E. Blunden (1936).

THE EVOLUTION OF KEATS'S POETRY, by C. L. Finney, 2 vols; Cambridge, Mass. (1936).

JOHN KEATS, by T. Saito; Tokyo (1936).

LIFE OF JOHN KEATS, by C. A. Brown, ed. with introduction and notes by D. H. Bodurtha and W. B. Pope (1937)
—first publication of reminiscences by Keats's friend Charles Brown.

ADONAIS: A Life of John Keats, by D. Hewlett (1937)
—revised and enlarged edition, entitled *A Life of John Keats*, 1949; 3rd revised ed., 1970.

KEATS AS DOCTOR AND PATIENT, by W. H. White (1938).

ROMANTIC POETRY AND THE FINE ARTS, by E. Blunden (1942)
—Warton Lecture on English Poetry, 1942. First printed in the *Proceedings of the British Academy*.

KEATS AND THE VICTORIANS: A Study of his influence and rise to fame, 1821–1895, by G. H. Ford (1944).

THE STYLISTIC DEVELOPMENT OF JOHN KEATS, by W. J. Bate; New York (1945).

THE IMAGERY OF KEATS AND SHELLEY: A Comparative study, by R. H. Fogle; Chapel Hill, N.C. (1949).

THE OPPOSING SELF: Nine essays in criticism, by L. Trilling; New York (1950)
—contains 'The Poet as Hero: Keats in his Letters'.

THE PREFIGURATIVE IMAGINATION OF KEATS: A Study of the beauty-truth identification and its implications, by N. F. Ford; Stanford (1951).

FANNY BRAWNE: A Biography, by Joanna Richardson (1952).
JOHN KEATS: The Living Year, 21 September, 1818 to 21 September, 1819, by Robert Gittings (1954).
THE MASK OF KEATS: A Study of problems, by R. Gittings (1956).
ON THE POETRY OF KEATS, by E. C. Pettet; Cambridge (1957)
—includes an extended analysis of *Endymion*.
JOHN KEATS: A Reassessment, ed. K. Muir; Liverpool (1958)
—essays by Kenneth Muir, Kenneth Allott, Miriam Allott, Arnold Davenport, R. T. Davies, Joan Grundy, and others.
THE QUEST FOR PERMANENCE: The Symbolism of Wordsworth, Shelley and Keats, by David Perkins; Cambridge, Mass. (1959).
KEATS AND REALITY, by John Bayley (1962)
—lively British Academy lecture.
JOHN KEATS, by W. J. Bate; Cambridge, Mass. (1963)
—highly distinguished and indispensable critical biography.
THE EVERLASTING SPELL: A Study of Keats and his friends, by Joanna Richardson (1963).
JOHN KEATS: The Making of a poet, by Aileen Ward (1963)
—biographical study, making suggestive use of the poems to illuminate Keats's character and temperament.
KEATS: A Collection of critical essays, ed. W. J. Bate; Englewood Cliffs (1964)
—in 'Twentieth Century Views' series.
THE KEATS INHERITANCE, by R. Gittings (1964)
—on the question of the Keats family's financial position.
AESTHETIC AND MYTH IN THE POETRY OF KEATS, by W. H. Evert; Princeton (1965).
JOHN KEATS: His life and writings, by Douglas Bush (1966)
—admirably succinct and informative introduction for the 'Masters of World Literature' series.
KEATS AND THE MIRROR OF ART, by I. Jack; Oxford (1967)
—an examination of Keats's cultural milieu, especially the influence of painters and art critics on his poetic development.
CRITICS ON KEATS, ed. J. O'Neill (1967)
—extracts from important critical works arranged in chronological order of Keats's writings.
JOHN KEATS, by R. Gittings (1968)
—impressively detailed biographical study.
TWENTIETH CENTURY INTERPRETATIONS OF KEATS'S ODES: A Collection of critical essays, ed. Jack Stillinger; Englewood Cliffs (1968)
—includes essays by M. H. Abrams, Kenneth Allott, W. J. Bate, Cleanth Brooks, David Perkins, Robert Penn Warren and others.
JOHN KEATS'S DREAM OF TRUTH, by John Jones (1969)

—on Keats and 'Romantic feeling'.

THE DAEMONIC IN THE POETRY OF JOHN KEATS, by Charles I. Patterson (1970)
—argues that the 'daemonic' in Keats is a non-malicious, pre-Christian, Greek conception and is in conflict with his personal feeling for the actual world.

KEATS AND HIS POETRY: A Study in development, by Morris Dickstein; Chicago (1971)
—explores the contrarieties in and the development of Keats's imagination through close reading of the texts, especially *Endymion*, the Odes, 'The Fall of Hyperion' and some minor poems.

KEATS AND HIS WORLD, by Timothy Hilton (1971)
—useful pictorial biography.

KEATS: The Critical heritage, ed. G. Matthews (1971)
—invaluable collection of early nineteenth-century and Victorian commentaries on Keats.

THE HOODWINKING OF MADELINE AND OTHER ESSAYS ON KEATS'S POEMS, by Jack Stillinger; Urbana (1971)
—offers an individual view of Keats's 'realism'.

KEATS THE POET, by Stuart M. Sperry; Princeton (1973)
—discusses the connexion between 'sensation' and 'thought' in Keats.

THE YOUNG ROMANTICS AND CRITICAL OPINION, 1807–1824: Poetry of Byron, Shelley and Keats as seen by their contemporary critics, by Theodore Redpath (1973)

KEATS AND EMBARRASSMENT, by Christopher Ricks; Oxford (1974)
—vivacious essay on evidence in Keats's poems and letters of his sensitivity to and intelligence about embarrassment.

THE TEXTS OF KEATS'S POEMS, by Jack Stillinger; Cambridge, Mass. (1974)
—offers a detailed analysis of textual problems in Keats and suggests principles for establishing a standard text. Reviewed by Miriam Allott, *The Times Literary Supplement*, 12 December 1975.

Note: Periodicals containing valuable regular contributions about Keats include *The Keats–Shelley Journal*, 1952– (see headnote and 'Bibliography' above) and the Bulletin of the Keats–Shelley Memorial, Rome (I, 1910; II, 1913, ed. Sir R. Rodd and H. N. Gay, republished 1962; III, [etc.] ed. D. Hewlett, 1950–).

recall the antithetical real world in the Nightingale ode,

> Where Beauty cannot keep her lustrous eyes,
>   Or new love pine at them beyond to-morrow,
>
> (29–30)

and lead into the plaintive invocation, 'O happy, happy love' (the epithet is equally insistent in the two earlier odes), which convey the total absence of happiness in the poet himself. Simultaneously the urn becomes remote,

> All breathing human passion far above,
>   That leaves a heart high-sorrowful and cloyed.   (28–9)

The entire stanza risks a damaging self-indulgence, from which Keats rescues himself by the brilliant innovation in his subsequent sestet which turns from the urn to the 'actual' world from which its figures came, a 'little town' where empty streets,

>   for evermore
>   Will silent be; and not a soul to tell
>   Why thou art desolate can e'er return,

a conception alien to the urn's creator but typical of the poet, who—this time obliquely—leads us back through the terms 'empty' and 'desolate' to his 'sole self'. From this he modulates into his attempted final summary, where the urn at first becomes no more than an 'Attic shape' covered with 'marble' —not 'warm' or 'panting'—figures. Yet his first delight still lingers with his new 'reflective' position, and the entire complex which 'teases us out of thought/As doth eternity' finds its only possible expressive outlet in the paradox 'Cold pastoral'. This closes the quartet and may be seen as the true imaginative climax of the poem. The sestet, with its too-much-discussed closing lines[1] represents Keats's final effort to subdue his doubts about the urn. He had opened *Endymion* with the line 'A thing of beauty is a joy for ever', a conception now reintroduced with the urn, again humanized, as 'a

[1] For a summary of the principal arguments, see *The Poems of John Keats*, ed. M. Allott, 1970, p. 537–8.

friend to man' who will console future generations 'in the midst of other woe than ours' with the one message it can offer. Its statement—

> 'Beauty is truth, truth beauty'—that is all
> Ye know on earth, and all ye need to know   (49–50)

—may be right or wrong. Keats does not say. It is the urn's offering and his decision to close with it brings a moment of repose.

There is a correspondence with these themes and ideas in the 'Ode on Melancholy', where the references to spring and early summer in the second of its three stanzas suggest that it too was written in May. The poem is perhaps the most concentrated expression of Keats's belief in the necessary relationship between joy and sorrow.

> Welcome joy and welcome sorrow,
>   Lethe's weed and Hermes' feather;
> Come today and come tomorrow,
>   I do love you both together!

are the opening lines of his 'little song' written in October 1818. Earlier he had described his 'pleasure-thermometer' in *Endymion*, Book I, as 'a first step' to his central theme, that is, 'the playing of different Natures with Joy and Sorrow', and had linked his 'Ode to Sorrow' in Book IV with his 'favourite Speculation', set out in a letter of November 1817 to his friend Benjamin Bailey: 'I am certain of nothing but of the holiness of the Heart's affections and the truth of Imagination —What the Imagination seizes as beauty must be truth . . . our Passions . . . are all in their sublime, creative of essential Beauty.' His youthful ode is attributed to the forlorn Indian maid. The burden of her song is

> Come then, Sorrow!
> Sweetest Sorrow!
> Like an own babe I nurse thee on my breast.
>   I thought to leave thee
>   And deceive thee,
> But now of all the world I love thee best   (IV, 279–84)

and it foreshadows his 1819 ode in connecting melancholy

with the perception of beauty and its transience. But it has nothing of the later poem's richness or economy. If I may repeat an earlier summary of mine,[1] Keats's 'argument' now runs, 'Melancholy is not to be found among thoughts of oblivion (stanza 1); it descends suddenly and is linked with beauty and its transience (stanza 2); it is associated with beauty, joy, pleasure and delight and is felt only by those who can experience these intensely (stanza 3)'. The three stanzas possess an imaginative consistency and must have 'come clear' after Keats had cancelled the false start of his original first stanza with its macabre and violent imagery,

> Though you should build a bark of dead men's bones,
> And rear a phantom gibbet for a mast,
> Stitch creeds together for a sail, with groans
> To fill it out, blood-stainèd and aghast;

the climax then being that one would still fail,

> To find the Melancholy—whether she
> Dreameth in any isle of Lethe dull . . .

The finished poem picks up this allusion in its opening lines,

> No, no, go not to Lethe, neither twist
> Wolf's-bane, tight-rooted, for its poisonous wine;

and thereafter unfolds images and ideas which are integral to Keats's May 1819 self-communings. He speaks of the death-moth as a 'mournful Psyche': the former has markings which resemble a human skull, and Psyche—the soul, as we know—was frequently represented as a butterfly. He rejects the drugged relief of oblivion—'shade to shade will come too drowsily/And drown the wakeful anguish of the soul . . .'—because, as he finds in the Nightingale ode, awareness, even if it is awareness of pain, is better than insentience, and, what is more, the 'wakeful anguish' fosters imaginative creativity just as the 'weeping cloud' of an April shower 'fosters the droop-headed flowers all'. He senses the close kinship of intense pleasure and intense pain: 'aching Pleasure nigh,/Turning to poison while the bee-mouth sips . . .'. And,

[1] See *The Poems of John Keats*, ed. cit., p. 358.

finally, from this keen sensitivity to suffering and change he seeks to evolve a statement whose imaginative order provides its own stay against impermanence. More explicit than elsewhere, and on another level from his young eroticism in *Endymion*, is his use, noticeable in the closing stanza, of sexual imagery as a paradigm for the inextricable relationship between joy and sorrow:

> Aye, in the very temple of Delight
> Veiled Melancholy has her sovran shrine.

As another critic has said,[1] the ensuing lines,

> Though seen of none save him whose strenuous tongue
> Can burst Joy's grape against his palate fine;
> His soul shall taste the sadness of her might,
> And be among her cloudy trophies hung,

indicates a recollection of *Troilus and Cressida*, III, ii, 19–24 (marked by Keats in his copy of Shakespeare),

> What will it be
> When that the wat'ry palates taste indeed
> Love's thrice-repured nectar? Death, I fear me;
> Sounding destruction; or some joy too fine,
> Too subtle-potent, tun'd too sharp in sweetness,
> For the capacity of my ruder powers,

and the parallel strengthens the felt presence of sexual elements in the stanza. Moreover the curve of feeling, familiar from the structure of the other odes and also found in other poems, which takes the poet from languor to intense sensation and out of this to another, sadder, and more anticlimactic, state of being, corresponds to the pattern of Keats's moods of poetic creativity.

It is the 'languor' alone which Keats celebrates in his 'Ode on Indolence'. The poem, not surprisingly, lacks the confident order of the other odes, which were written in obedience to a more urgent creative impulse. Keats, it seems, found difficulty even in deciding on the final arrangement of his

---

[1] Douglas Bush, *John Keats*, 1966, p. 147.